Maintainable JavaScript

Nicholas C. Zakas

O'REILLY®

Beijing · Boston · Farnham · Sebastopol · Tokyo

Maintainable JavaScript
by Nicholas C. Zakas

Published by O'Reilly Media, Inc., 1005 Gravenstein Highway North, Sebastopol, CA 95472.

O'Reilly books may be purchased for educational, business, or sales promotional use. Online editions are also available for most titles (*http://safaribooksonline.com*). For more information, contact our corporate/institutional sales department: 800-998-9938 or *corporate@oreilly.com*.

Editor: Mary Treseler		**Indexer:** Lucie Haskins	
Production Editor: Holly Bauer		**Cover Designer:** Karen Montgomery	
Copyeditor: Nancy Kotary		**Interior Designer:** David Futato	
Proofreader: Linley Dolby		**Illustrator:** Rebecca Demarest	

May 2012:   First Edition.

Revision History for the First Edition:
  2012-05-09   First release
  2018-01-26   Second release

See *http://oreilly.com/catalog/errata.csp?isbn=9781449327682* for release details.

Nutshell Handbook, the Nutshell Handbook logo, and the O'Reilly logo are registered trademarks of O'Reilly Media, Inc. *Maintainable JavaScript*, the image of a Greek tortoise, and related trade dress are trademarks of O'Reilly Media, Inc.

Many of the designations used by manufacturers and sellers to distinguish their products are claimed as trademarks. Where those designations appear in this book, and O'Reilly Media, Inc., was aware of a trademark claim, the designations have been printed in caps or initial caps.

ISBN: 978-1-449-32768-2

[LSI]

1336581596

Table of Contents

Part II.   Programming Practices

Part III.   Automation

Introduction

The professionalization of web development has been a difficult journey because of our disparate beginnings. Even those who end up at large companies such as Yahoo! inevitably began on their own, hacking around. Perhaps you were even "the web guy" at a small company and could do pretty much whatever you wanted. When the large companies started tapping this previously undiscovered resource, it brought a lot of hackers into a corporate environment, where they were met with constraints. No longer a lone soldier in a small battle, all of these self-taught, self-directed individuals had to figure out how to work within a team environment.

I learned JavaScript the way many did in the late 1990s: I taught myself. Because Java-Script was so new, educational resources were scarce. I, like many other developers, learned by exploring the intricacies of Internet Explorer and Netscape Navigator on my own. I experimented, theorized, and experimented again until I discovered how things worked. Luckily for me, this curiosity and diligence turned into my first job.

For the first five years of my professional career, I was "the JavaScript guy." No one in either of my first two companies could match my depth of knowledge in JavaScript and web development in general. All problems, from very simple to very difficult, ended up on my desk to solve by myself. It was both empowering as a fresh-from-college kid and terrifying because I had no one to bounce ideas off of or anyone to ask for help if I got stuck. I did the best that I could, knowing that I was the only one who could do it.

During those five years, I honed my craft. I came up with ways of doing things that made sense to me and my workflow. I didn't have to worry about what anyone else thought of my code, because no one had enough knowledge to code review or fix what I had written. I was a hacker in its purest sense: I wrote code the way I wanted and wouldn't hear of changing it.

In year six of my professional career, I switched jobs and ended up on a team where everyone was expected to contribute code in all aspects of the project. No longer able to focus on JavaScript and web development, I found myself writing server-side code and SQL queries most of the time. Meanwhile, traditionally backend-focused developers were being forced to write web code. This experience really opened my eyes: the way I used to write code wasn't the way the rest of the team wrote code, and that was a problem.

I quickly realized that to be more effective on the team, I had to start writing code the way the rest of the team wrote code. Server-side code and SQL were a bit alien to me, so I adopted the patterns of those around me who knew what they were doing. At the same time, I started talking to the other engineers about adopting coding patterns for HTML, CSS, and JavaScript. I even added JavaScript linting into the build process to enforce our standards—the first test of web code ever at the company. And soon, the team was working as a well-oiled machine.

When I arrived at Yahoo! in 2006, I came with a specific idea of how things should work when I got there. What I found was a completely different animal altogether. The My Yahoo! team, the first team I worked on, was much larger than any I had worked on before. There were already pseudoguidelines in place, and I had a lot to learn. New technologies, new processes, and new tools were presented to me on a daily basis. I was overwhelmed and resigned myself to spending some time learning about this new environment and soaking up as much knowledge as I could from my colleagues.

After a few months, I started to find problems. The processes I had finally become accustomed to weren't working all the time. There were a lot of people doing things in different ways, and that caused bugs. My manager, noticing this trend, pulled me aside one day and said he'd like me to take lead on cleaning up our development. His words, still inspiring to me, were, "When you write code, things just work—they rarely have bugs. I want everyone to write code like you do." And with that, I set out to add some structure to the My Yahoo! frontend development team.

The success I had working on the My Yahoo! team ultimately led to my being chosen as the frontend tech lead for the Yahoo! home page redesign of 2008. This assignment really put my organizational and code quality skills to the test, as we had more than 20 frontend engineers working with the same code. After a few months of learning and adjusting, the team reached such a high level of productivity and quality that many were amazed. Not only did all code look remarkably similar regardless of who wrote it, but most developers were capable of quickly switching to someone else's work to fix bugs or implement new features. What we accomplished as an engineering team over the course of a couple years is still one of the highlights of my career.

It was during my time at Yahoo!, working on large teams, that I accumulated the tips and techniques discussed in this book. The topics highlight how I transformed myself from a hacker, always doing things his own way, to a software engineer, a team player who gave up some of himself so that the team could function at a higher level. And that's really what this book is about: how to write JavaScript as part of a team.

The hard truth that developers often don't understand is that we spend most of our time *maintaining* code. It's rare that you get to open up a text editor and start writing code from scratch. Most of the time, you're building on code that's already there. Writing code in a maintainable way allows you, and others who will work on your code after you, to easily pick up where the code leaves off. As I used to always tell my colleagues at Yahoo!: "When you come to work, you're not writing code for you, you're writing code for those who come after you."

This book is a collection and discussion of code conventions for JavaScript. One of the most popular code convention documents, Code Conventions for the Java Programming Language, lists the following reasons that code conventions are important:

- Eighty percent of the lifetime cost of a piece of software goes to maintenance.
- Hardly any software is maintained for its whole life by the original author.
- Code conventions improve the readability of the software, allowing engineers to understand new code more quickly and thoroughly.
- If you ship your source code as a product, you need to make sure that it is as well packaged and clean as any other product you create.

This reasoning still rings true today. The conventions discussed in this book are all aimed at helping you and your team write JavaScript in the most effective way possible.

Because you're reading this book, you probably are open to the suggestions contained herein. Keep in mind that these techniques are really aimed at a multideveloper environment in which there are many engineers all working on the same code. Being a part of a team means making decisions that are best not for you, but for the team as a whole. And that sometimes means sacrificing your preferences, your ideas, and your ego. What you receive in return is a high-functioning team capable of doing great things, and I hope this book will help you along that road.

Preface

Conventions Used in This Book

The following typographical conventions are used in this book:

Italic
> Indicates new terms, URLs, email addresses, filenames, and file extensions.

`Constant width`
> Used for program listings, as well as within paragraphs to refer to program elements such as variable or function names, databases, data types, environment variables, statements, and keywords.

`Constant width bold`
> Shows commands or other text that should be typed literally by the user.

`Constant width italic`
> Shows text that should be replaced with user-supplied values or by values determined by context.

This icon signifies a tip, suggestion, or general note.

This icon indicates a warning or caution.

Using Code Examples

This book is here to help you get your job done. In general, you may use the code in this book in your programs and documentation. You do not need to contact us for permission unless you're reproducing a significant portion of the code. For example, writing a program that uses several chunks of code from this book does not require permission. Selling or distributing a CD-ROM of examples from O'Reilly books does require permission. Answering a question by citing this book and quoting example code does not require permission. Incorporating a significant amount of example code from this book into your product's documentation does require permission.

We appreciate, but do not require, attribution. An attribution usually includes the title, author, publisher, and ISBN. For example: *Maintainable JavaScript* by Nicholas Zakas (O'Reilly). Copyright 2012 Nicholas Zakas, 978-1-449-32768-2.

If you feel your use of code examples falls outside fair use or the permission given above, feel free to contact us at *permissions@oreilly.com*.

Safari® Books Online

 Safari Books Online (*www.safaribooksonline.com*) is an on-demand digital library that delivers expert content in both book and video form from the world's leading authors in technology and business.

Technology professionals, software developers, web designers, and business and creative professionals use Safari Books Online as their primary resource for research, problem solving, learning, and certification training.

Safari Books Online offers a range of product mixes and pricing programs for organizations, government agencies, and individuals. Subscribers have access to thousands of books, training videos, and prepublication manuscripts in one fully searchable database from publishers like O'Reilly Media, Prentice Hall Professional, Addison-Wesley Professional, Microsoft Press, Sams, Que, Peachpit Press, Focal Press, Cisco Press, John Wiley & Sons, Syngress, Morgan Kaufmann, IBM Redbooks, Packt, Adobe Press, FT Press, Apress, Manning, New Riders, McGraw-Hill, Jones & Bartlett, Course Technology, and dozens more. For more information about Safari Books Online, please visit us online.

How to Contact Us

Please address comments and questions concerning this book to the publisher:

O'Reilly Media, Inc.
1005 Gravenstein Highway North
Sebastopol, CA 95472
800-998-9938 (in the United States or Canada)
707-829-0515 (international or local)
707-829-0104 (fax)

We have a web page for this book, where we list errata, examples, and any additional information. You can access this page at:

http://oreil.ly/maintainable_js

To comment or ask technical questions about this book, send email to:

bookquestions@oreilly.com

For more information about our books, courses, conferences, and news, see our website at *http://www.oreilly.com*.

Find us on Facebook: *http://facebook.com/oreilly*

Follow us on Twitter: *http://twitter.com/oreillymedia*

Watch us on YouTube: *http://www.youtube.com/oreillymedia*

PART I

Style Guidelines

"Programs are meant to be read by humans and only incidentally for computers to execute." —Donald Knuth

When a team is brought together for the first time, everyone brings with them their own ideas about how code should be written. After all, each team member comes from a different background. Some may come from one-man shops where they could do whatever they wanted; others may have been on different teams that had particular ways of doing things that they liked (or hated). Everyone has an opinion about how code should be written, and it usually falls in line with how that individual would personally write it. Establishing style guidelines should always come as early in the process as possible.

 The terms "style guidelines" and "code conventions" are often used interchangeably. Style guidelines are a type of code convention aimed at the layout of code within a file. Code conventions can also include programming practices, file and directory layout, and commenting. This book is actually a collection and discussion of code conventions for JavaScript.

Why Style Guidelines?

Figuring out style guidelines is a process that typically takes longer than it should. Everyone has an opinion and, when you're going to be spending eight hours a day writing code, all programmers want to do so in a way that is comfortable to them. It takes some compromise within the team and a strong leader to move the conversation forward. Once established, style guidelines allow the team to work at a much higher level, because all code looks the same.

Having all code look the same is incredibly important on a team, because it allows:

- Any developer to work on any file regardless of who wrote it. There's no need to spend time reformatting or deciphering the logic of the file, because it looks the same as everything else. If you've ever opened a file and immediately fixed all the indentation before starting your work, you can understand the time savings consistency provides when working on a large project.

- Errors become more obvious. If all code looks the same, and you come across some code that doesn't, you've likely found a problem.

It's no wonder that large companies around the world have published style guidelines either internally or publicly.

Style guidelines are a personal thing and must be developed within a team to be effective. This section of the book lists recommended focus areas for the development of your JavaScript code conventions. In some cases, it's impossible to tell you that one guideline is better than another, because some are just a matter of preference. Rather than trying to force my preferences upon you, this chapter highlights important aspects that should be covered in your style guidelines. My personal code style guidelines for JavaScript are included in Appendix A.

Useful Tools

Developing coding guidelines is difficult enough—enforcing them is a whole other story. Establishing agreement among your team and performing code reviews will get you part of the way there, but everyone slips up once in a while. Tools help to keep everyone on track. There are two extremely useful tools for style guidelines: JSLint and JSHint.

JSLint (*http://www.jslint.com*) was written by Douglas Crockford as a general code-quality tool for JavaScript. It began as a simple utility for finding common problematic JavaScript patterns. Over the years, it has evolved into a tool that not only finds potential errors but also warns about stylistic issues in your code.

Crockford wrote his ideas about JavaScript style in three different pieces:

- "The Elements of JavaScript Style, Part 1" (*http://javascript.crockford.com/style1 .html*) covers basic patterns and syntax.
- "The Elements of JavaScript Style, Part 2" (*http://javascript.crockford.com/style2 .html*) covers common JavaScript idioms.
- "Code Conventions for the JavaScript Programming Language" (*http://javascript .crockford.com/code.html*) is a more exhaustive resource that highlights pieces from the first two, with the addition of smaller style guidelines.

JSLint now incorporates many of Crockford's style preferences directly, frequently without the ability to turn them off. So JSLint is a good tool—provided that you agree with Crockford's style guidelines.

JSHint (*http://www.jshint.com*) is a fork of JSLint that is maintained by Anton Kovalyov. The goal of JSHint is to provide a more customizable code quality and style guideline tool for JavaScript. With the exception of syntax errors, it's possible to turn off nearly all warnings in JSHint, allowing you to fully customize the messages you receive about your code. Kovalyov encourages participation and contribution to JSHint through the source code repository at GitHub (*https://github.com/jshint/jshint*).

Integrating one of these tools into your build process is a good way to start enforcing code conventions as well as catching potential errors in your JavaScript code.

CHAPTER 1

Basic Formatting

At the core of a style guide are basic formatting rules. These rules govern how the code is written at a high level. Similar to the ruled paper used in schools to teach writing, basic formatting rules guide developers toward writing code in a particular style. These rules often contain information about syntax that you may not have considered, but every piece is important in creating a coherent piece of code.

Indentation Levels

The first decision to be made about your JavaScript style guidelines (and indeed, about those of most languages) is how to handle indentation. This is one of those topics on which debates can last for hours; indentation is about as close to religion as software engineers get. However, it is quite important to establish indentation guidelines up front, lest developers fall into the classic problem of reindenting every file they open before starting to work. Consider a file that looks like this (indentation has been intentionally changed for demonstration purposes):

```
if (wl && wl.length) {
        for (i = 0, l = wl.length; i < l; ++i) {
        p = wl[i];
        type = Y.Lang.type(r[p]);
        if (s.hasOwnProperty(p)) { if (merge && type == 'object') {

    Y.mix(r[p], s[p]);
} else if (ov || !(p in r)) {
                r[p] = s[p];
            }
        }
    }
}
```

Just looking at this code quickly is difficult. The indentation isn't uniform, so it appears that the `else` applies to the `if` statement on the first line. However, closer inspection reveals that the `else` actually applies to the `if` statement on line 5. The most likely culprit is a mixture of indentation styles from several different developers. This is precisely why indentation guidelines exist. Properly indented, this code becomes much easier to understand:

```
if (wl && wl.length) {
    for (i = 0, l = wl.length; i < l; ++i) {
        p = wl[i];
        type = Y.Lang.type(r[p]);
        if (s.hasOwnProperty(p)) {
            if (merge && type == 'object') {
                Y.mix(r[p], s[p]);
            } else if (ov || !(p in r)) {
                r[p] = s[p];
            }
        }
    }
}
```

Ensuring proper indentation is the first step—this particular piece of code has other maintainability issues discussed later in this chapter.

As with most style guidelines, there is no universal agreement on how to accomplish indentation in code. There are two schools of thought:

Use tabs for indentation

Each indentation level is represented by a single tab character. So indents of one level are one tab character, second-level indentation is two tab characters, and so on. There are two main advantages to this approach. First, there is a one-to-one mapping between tab characters and indentation levels, making it logical. Second, text editors can be configured to display tabs as different sizes, so developers who like smaller indents can configure their editors that way, and those who like larger indents can work their way, too. The main disadvantage of tabs for indentation is that systems interpret them differently. You may find that opening the file in one editor or system looks quite different than in another, which can be frustrating for someone looking for consistency. These differences, some argue, result in each developer looking at the same code differently, and that isn't how a team should operate.

Use spaces for indentation

Each indentation level is made up of multiple space characters. Within this realm of thinking, there are three popular approaches: two spaces per indent, four spaces per indent, and eight spaces per indent. These approaches all can be traced back to style guidelines for various programming languages. In practice, many teams opt to go with a four-space indent as a compromise between those who want two spaces and those who want eight spaces. The main advantage of using spaces for indentation is that the files are treated exactly the same in all editors and all systems. Text editors can be configured to insert spaces when the Tab key is pressed. That means all developers have the same view of the code. The main disadvantage of using spaces for indentation is that it is easy for a single developer to create formatting issues by having a misconfigured text editor.

Though some may argue that one indentation approach or another is superior, it all boils down to a matter of preference within the team. For reference, here are some indentation guidelines from various style guides:

- The jQuery Core Style Guide specifies indents as tabs.
- Douglas Crockford's Code Conventions for the JavaScript Programming Language specifies indents as four spaces.
- The SproutCore Style Guide specifies indents as two spaces.
- The Google JavaScript Style Guide specifies indents as two spaces.
- The Dojo Style Guide specifies indents as tabs.

I recommend using four spaces per indentation level. Many text editors have this level as a default if you decide to make the Tab key insert spaces instead. I've found that two spaces don't provide enough visual distinction for my eyes.

 Even though the choice of tabs or spaces is a preference, it is very important not to mix them. Doing so leads to horrible file layout and requires cleanup work, as in the very first example in this section.

Statement Termination

One of the interesting, and most confusing, aspects of JavaScript is that statements may be terminated either with a newline or with a semicolon. This breaks from the tradition of other C-like languages such as C++ and Java, which require semicolons. Both of the following examples are therefore valid JavaScript.

```
// Valid
var name = "Nicholas";
function sayName() {
    alert(name);
}

// Valid but not recommended
var name = "Nicholas"
function sayName() {
    alert(name)
}
```

The omission of semicolons works in JavaScript due to a mechanism known as automatic semicolon insertion (ASI). ASI looks for places in the code where a semicolon is appropriate and inserts one if not found. In many cases, ASI guesses correctly and there isn't a problem. However, the rules of ASI are complex and difficult to remember, which is why I recommend using semicolons. Consider the following:

```
// Original Code
function getData() {
    return
    {
        title: "Maintainable JavaScript",
        author: "Nicholas C. Zakas"
    }
}

// The way the parser sees it
function getData() {
    return;
    {
        title: "Maintainable JavaScript",
        author: "Nicholas C. Zakas"
    };
}
```

In this example, the function getData() is intended to return an object containing some data. However, the newline after return causes a semicolon to be inserted, which causes the function to return undefined. The function can be fixed by moving the opening brace on to the same line as return.

```
// Works correctly, even without semicolons
function getData() {
    return {
        title: "Maintainable JavaScript",
        author: "Nicholas C. Zakas"
    }
}
```

There are scenarios where ASI may be applied, and I've found limiting ASI to help reduce errors. The errors are typically caused by misunderstanding how ASI works and assuming that a semicolon will be inserted when it will not. I have found that many developers, especially inexperienced ones, have an easier time using semicolons than omitting them.

Semicolon usage is recommended by Douglas Crockford's Code Conventions for the JavaScript Programming Language (hereafter referred to as "Crockford's Code Conventions"), the jQuery Core Style Guide, the Google JavaScript Style Guide, and the Dojo Style Guide. Both JSLint and JSHint will warn by default when semicolons are missing.

Line Length

Closely related to the topic of indentation is line length. Developers find it hard to work on code in which the lines are long enough to require horizontal scrolling. Even with today's large monitors, keeping line length reasonable greatly improves developer productivity. Code convention documents for many languages prescribe that lines of code should be no longer than 80 characters. This length comes from a time when text editors had a maximum of 80 columns in which to display text, so longer lines would either wrap in unexpected ways or disappear off the side of the editor. Today's text editors are quite a bit more sophisticated than those of 20 years ago, yet 80-character lines are still quite popular. Here are some common line length recommendations:

1. Code Conventions for the Java Programming Language specifies a line length of 80 characters for source code and 70 characters for documentation.
2. The Android Code Style Guidelines for Contributors specifies a line length of 100 characters.
3. The Unofficial Ruby Usage Guide specifies a line length of 80 characters.
4. The Python Style Guidelines specifies a line length of 79 characters.

Line length is less frequently found in JavaScript style guidelines, but Crockford's Code Conventions specifies a line length of 80 characters. I also prefer to keep line length at 80 characters.

Line Breaking

When a line reaches the maximum character length, it must be manually split into two lines. Line breaking is typically done after an operator, and the next line is indented two levels. For example (indents are four spaces):

```
// Good: Break after operator, following line indented two levels
callAFunction(document, element, window, "some string value", true, 123,
        navigator);

// Bad: Following line indented only one level
callAFunction(document, element, window, "some string value", true, 123,
    navigator);

// Bad: Break before operator
callAFunction(document, element, window, "some string value", true, 123
        , navigator);
```

In this example, the comma is an operator and so should come last on the preceding line. This placement is important because of ASI mechanism, which may close a statement at the end of a line in certain situations. By always ending with an operator, ASI won't come into play and introduce possible errors.

The same line-breaking pattern should be used for statements as well:

```
if (isLeapYear && isFebruary && day == 29 && itsYourBirthday &&
        noPlans) {

    waitAnotherFourYears();
}
```

Here, the control condition of the `if` statement is split onto a second line after the `&&` operator. Note that the body of the `if` statement is still indented only one level, allowing for easier reading.

There is one exception to this rule. When assigning a value to a variable, the wrapped line should appear immediately under the first part of the assignment. For example:

```
var result = something + anotherThing + yetAnotherThing + somethingElse +
            anotherSomethingElse;
```

This code aligns the variable `anotherSomethingElse` with `something` on the first line, ensuring readability and providing context for the wrapped line.

Blank Lines

An often overlooked aspect of code style is the use of blank lines. In general, code should look like a series of paragraphs rather than one continuous blob of text. Blank lines should be used to separate related lines of code from unrelated lines of code. The example from the earlier section "Indentation Levels" on page 5 is perfect for adding some extra blank lines to improve readability. Here's the original:

```
if (wl && wl.length) {
    for (i = 0, l = wl.length; i < l; ++i) {
        p = wl[i];
        type = Y.Lang.type(r[p]);
        if (s.hasOwnProperty(p)) {
            if (merge && type == 'object') {
                Y.mix(r[p], s[p]);
            } else if (ov || !(p in r)) {
                r[p] = s[p];
            }
        }
    }
}
```

And here is the example rewritten with a few blank lines inserted:

```
if (wl && wl.length) {

    for (i = 0, l = wl.length; i < l; ++i) {
        p = wl[i];
        type = Y.Lang.type(r[p]);

        if (s.hasOwnProperty(p)) {

            if (merge && type == 'object') {
                Y.mix(r[p], s[p]);
            } else if (ov || !(p in r)) {
                r[p] = s[p];
            }
        }
    }
}
```

The guideline followed in this example is to add a blank line before each flow control statement, such as `if` and `for`. Doing so allows you to more easily read the statements. In general, it's a good idea to also add blank lines:

- Between methods
- Between the local variables in a method and its first statement
- Before a multiline or single-line comment
- Between logical sections inside a method to improve readability

None of the major style guides provide specific advice about blank lines, though Crockford's Code Conventions does suggest using them judiciously.

Naming

> "There are only two hard problems in Computer Science: cache invalidation and naming things." —Phil Karlton

Most of the code you write involves variables and functions, so determining naming conventions for those variables and functions is quite important to a comprehensive understanding of the code. JavaScript's core, ECMAScript, is written using a convention called *camel case*. Camel-case names begin with a lowercase letter and each subsequent word begins with an uppercase letter. For example:

```
var thisIsMyName;
var anotherVariable;
var aVeryLongVariableName;
```

Generally speaking, you should always use a naming convention that follows the core language that you're using, so camel case is the way most JavaScript developers name their variables and functions. The Google JavaScript Style Guide, the SproutCore Style Guide, and the Dojo Style Guide all specify use of camel case in most situations.

Even with the general naming convention of camel case in place, some more specific styles of naming are typically specified.

 Another notation called Hungarian notation was popular for JavaScript around the year 2000. This notation involved prepending a variable type identifier at the beginning of a name, such as `sName` for a string and `iCount` for an integer. This style has now fallen out of favor and isn't recommended by any of the major style guides.

Variables and Functions

Variable names are always camel case and should begin with a noun. Beginning with a noun helps to differentiate variables from functions, which should begin with a verb. Here are some examples:

```
// Good
var count = 10;
var myName = "Nicholas";
var found = true;

// Bad: Easily confused with functions
var getCount = 10;
var isFound = true;

// Good
function getName() {
    return myName;
}

// Bad: Easily confused with variable
function theName() {
    return myName;
}
```

The naming of variables is more art than science, but in general, you should try to make the variable names as short as possible to get the point across. Try to make the variable name indicate the data type of its value. For example, the names `count`, `length`, and `size` suggest the data type is a number, and names such as `name`, `title`, and `message` suggest the data type is a string. Single-character variable names such as `i`, `j`, and `k` are typically reserved for use in loops. Using names that suggest the data type makes your code easier to understand by others as well as yourself.

Meaningless names should be avoided. Names such as `foo`, `bar`, and `temp`, despite being part of the developer's toolbox, don't give any meaning to variables. There's no way for another developer to understand what the variable is being used for without understanding all of the context.

For function and method names, the first word should always be a verb, and there are some common conventions used for that verb:

Verb	Meaning
can	Function returns a boolean
has	Function returns a boolean
is	Function returns a boolean
get	Function returns a nonboolean
set	Function is used to save a value

Following these conventions as a starting point makes code much more readable. Here are some examples:

```
if (isEnabled()) {
    setName("Nicholas");
}
```

```
if (getName() === "Nicholas") {
    doSomething();
}
```

Although none of the popular style guides go to this level of detail regarding function names, these are pseudostandards among JavaScript developers and can be found in many popular libraries.

 jQuery quite obviously doesn't follow this naming convention for functions, partly due to how methods are used in jQuery, as many act as both getters and setters. For example, $("body").attr("class") returns the value of the class attribute, and $("body").attr("class", "selected") sets the value of the class attribute. Despite this, I still recommend using verbs for function names.

Constants

JavaScript had no formal concept of constants prior to ECMAScript 6. However, that didn't stop developers from defining variables to be used as constants. To differentiate normal variables (those meant to have changing values) and constants (variables that are initialized to a value and never change), a common naming convention evolved. The convention comes from C and uses all uppercase letters with underscores separating words, as in:

```
var MAX_COUNT = 10;
var URL = "http://www.nczonline.net/";
```

Keep in mind that these are just variables using a different naming convention, so it's still possible to overwrite the values. Normal variables and constants are easily differentiated by using this very different convention. Consider the following example:

```
if (count < MAX_COUNT) {
    doSomething();
}
```

In this code, it's easy to tell that count is a variable that may change and MAX_COUNT is a variable that is intended to never change. This convention adds another level of semantics to the underlying code.

The Google JavaScript Style Guide, the SproutCore Style Guide, and the Dojo Style Guide specify that constants should be formatted in this manner (the Dojo Style Guide also allows constants to be specified as Pascal case; see the following section).

Constructors

JavaScript constructors are simply functions that are used to create objects via the new operator. The language contains many built-in constructors, such as Object and RegExp, and developers can add their own constructors to create new types. As with other naming conventions, constructors follow the native language, so constructors are formatted using Pascal case.

Pascal case is the same as camel case except that the initial letter is uppercase. So instead of `anotherName`, you would use `AnotherName`. Doing so helps to differentiate constructors from both variables and nonconstructor functions. Constructor names also are typically nouns, as they are used to create instances of a type. Here are some examples:

```
// Good
function Person(name) {
    this.name = name;
}

Person.prototype.sayName = function() {
    alert(this.name);
};

var me = new Person("Nicholas");
```

Following this convention also makes it easier to spot errors later. You know that functions whose names are nouns in Pascal case must be preceded by the `new` operator. Consider the following:

```
var me = Person("Nicholas");
var you = getPerson("Michael");
```

Here, line 1 should jump out as a problem to you, but line 2 looks okay according to the conventions already laid out in this chapter.

Crockford's Code Conventions, the Google JavaScript Style Guide, and the Dojo Style Guide all recommend this practice. JSLint will warn if a constructor is found without an initial uppercase letter or if a constructor function is used without the `new` operator. JSHint will warn if a constructor is found without an initial uppercase letter only if you add the special `newcap` option.

Literal Values

JavaScript has several types of primitive literal values: strings, numbers, booleans, `null`, and `undefined`. There are also object literals and array literals. Of these, only booleans are self-explanatory in their use. All of the other types require a little bit of thought as to how they should be used for optimum clarity.

Strings

Strings are unique in JavaScript, in that they can be indicated by either double quotes or single quotes. For example:

```
// Valid JavaScript
var name = "Nicholas says, \"Hi.\"";
```

```
// Also valid JavaScript
var name = 'Nicholas says, "Hi"';
```

Unlike other languages such as Java and PHP, there is absolutely no functional difference between using double quotes and single quotes for strings. They behave exactly the same, except that the string delimiter must be escaped. So in this example, in the string using double quotes, we had to escape the double quote characters, and in the string using single quotes, we did not. What matters is that you pick a single style and stick with it throughout the code base.

Crockford's Code Conventions and the jQuery Core Style Guide both specify the use of double quotes for strings. The Google JavaScript Style Guide specifies the use of single quotes for strings. I prefer using double quotes, because I tend to switch back and forth between writing Java and JavaScript frequently. Because Java uses only double quotes for strings, I find it easier to switch between contexts by maintaining that convention in JavaScript. This sort of issue should always be a consideration when developing conventions: do what makes it easiest for engineers to do their jobs.

Another aspect of strings is the hidden ability to create multiline strings. This feature was never specified as part of the JavaScript language but still works in all engines:

```
// Bad
var longString = "Here's the story, of a man \
named Brady.";
```

Although this is technically invalid JavaScript syntax, it effectively creates a multiline string in code. This technique is generally frowned upon because it relies on a language quirk rather than a language feature, and it is explicitly forbidden in the Google JavaScript Style Guide. Instead of using multiline strings, split the string into multiple strings and concatenate them together:

```
// Good
var longString = "Here's the story, of a man " +
                 "named Brady.";
```

Numbers

The number type is unique to JavaScript, because all types of numbers—integers and floats—are stored in the same data type. There are also several literal formats for numbers to represent various numeric formats. Most formats are fine to use, but some are quite problematic:

```
// Integer
var count = 10;

// Decimal
var price = 10.0;
var price = 10.00;

// Bad Decimal: Hanging decimal point
var price = 10.;
```

```
// Bad Decimal: Leading decimal point
var price = .1;

// Bad: Octal (base 8) is deprecated
var num = 010;

// Hexadecimal (base 16)
var num = 0xA2;

// E-notation
var num = 1e23;
```

The first two problematic formats are the hanging decimal point, such as `10.`, and the leading decimal point, such as `.1`. Each format has the same problem: it's hard to know if the omission of values before or after the decimal point are intentional. It could very well be that the developer mistyped the value. It's a good idea to always include digits before and after the decimal point to avoid any confusion. These two formats are explicitly forbidden in the Dojo Style Guide. Both JSLint and JSHint warn when one of these two patterns is found.

The last problematic numeric format is the octal format. JavaScript's support of octal numbers has long been a source of error and confusion. The literal number `010` doesn't represent 10; it represents 8 in octal. Most developers aren't familiar with octal format, and there's rarely a reason to use it, so the best approach is to disallow octal literals in code. Although not called out in any of the popular style guides, both JSLint and JSHint will warn when they come across an octal literal.

Null

The special value `null` is often misunderstood and confused with `undefined`. This value should be used in just a few cases:

- To initialize a variable that may later be assigned an object value
- To compare against an initialized variable that may or may not have an object value
- To pass into a function where an object is expected
- To return from a function where an object is expected

There are also some cases in which `null` should not be used:

- Do not use `null` to test whether an argument was supplied.
- Do not test an uninitialized variable for the value `null`.

Here are some examples:

```
// Good
var person = null;

// Good
function getPerson() {
```

```
    if (condition) {
        return new Person("Nicholas");
    } else {
        return null;
    }
}

// Good
var person = getPerson();
if (person !== null) {
    doSomething();
}

// Bad: Testing against uninitialized variable
var person;
if (person != null) {
    doSomething();
}

// Bad: Testing to see whether an argument was passed
function doSomething(arg1, arg2, arg3, arg4) {
    if (arg4 != null) {
        doSomethingElse();
    }
}
```

The best way to think about null is as a placeholder for an object. These rules are not covered by any major style guide but are important for overall maintainability.

 A longer discussion around the pitfalls of null is found in Chapter 8.

Undefined

The special value undefined is frequently confused with null. Part of the confusion is that null == undefined is true. However, these two values have two very different uses. Variables that are not initialized have an initial value of undefined, which essentially means the variable is waiting to have a real value. For example:

```
// Bad
var person;
console.log(person === undefined);    //true
```

Despite this working, I recommend avoiding the use of undefined in code. This value is frequently confused with the typeof operator returning the string "undefined" for a value. In fact, the behavior is quite confusing, because typeof will return the string "undefined" both for variables whose value is undefined and for undeclared variables. Example:

```
// foo is not declared
var person;
console.log(typeof person);    //"undefined"
console.log(typeof foo);       //"undefined"
```

In this example, both `person` and `foo` cause `typeof` to return "undefined" even though they behave very different in almost every other way (trying to use `foo` in a statement will cause an error, but using `person` will not).

By avoiding the use of the special value `undefined`, you effectively keep the meaning of `typeof` returning "undefined" to a single case: when a variable hasn't been declared. If you're using a variable that may or may not be assigned an object value later on, initialize it to `null`:

```
// Good
var person = null;
console.log(person === null);    //true
```

Setting a variable to `null` initially indicates your intent for that variable; it should eventually contain an object. The `typeof` operator returns "object" for a `null` value, so it can be differentiated from `undefined`.

Object Literals

Object literals are a popular way to create new objects with a specific set of properties, as opposed to explicitly creating a new instance of `Object` and then adding properties. For example, this pattern is rarely used:

```
// Bad
var book = new Object();
book.title = "Maintainable JavaScript";
book.author = "Nicholas C. Zakas";
```

Object literals allow you to specify all of the properties within two curly braces. Literals effectively perform the same tasks as their nonliteral counterparts, just with more compact syntax.

When defining object literals, it's typical to include the opening brace on the first line, then each property-value pair on its own line, indented one level, then the closing brace on its own line. For example:

```
// Good
var book = {
    title: "Maintainable JavaScript",
    author: "Nicholas C. Zakas"
};
```

This is the format most commonly seen in open source JavaScript code. Though it's not commonly documented, the Google JavaScript Style Guide does recommend this format. Crockford's Code Conventions recommends using object literals over the `Object` constructor but does not specify a particular format.

Array Literals

Array literals, as with object literals, are a more compact way of defining arrays in JavaScript. Explicitly using the `Array` constructor, as in this example, is generally frowned upon:

```
// Bad
var colors = new Array("red", "green", "blue");
var numbers = new Array(1, 2, 3, 4);
```

Instead of using the `Array` constructor, you can use two square brackets and include the initial members of the array:

```
// Good
var colors = [ "red", "green", "blue" ];
var numbers = [ 1, 2, 3, 4 ];
```

This pattern is widely used and quite common in JavaScript. It is also recommended by the Google JavaScript Style Guide and Crockford's Code Conventions.

CHAPTER 2

Comments

Comments are often the least popular part of coding. They're dangerously close to documentation, which is the last thing any developer wants to spend time doing. However, comments are incredibly important for the overall maintainability of the code. Opening a file without any comments may seem like a fun adventure, but when there are deadlines to meet, this task turns into torture. Appropriately written comments help tell the story of code, allowing other developers to drop into a part of the story without needing to hear the beginning. Style guidelines don't always cover commenting styles, but I consider them important enough to warrant their own section.

JavaScript supports two different types of comments: single-line and multiline.

Single-Line Comments

Single-line comments are created by using two slashes and end at the end of the line:

```
// Single-line comment
```

Many prefer to include a space after the two slashes to offset the comment text. There are three ways in which a single-line comment is used:

- On its own line, explaining the line following the comment. The line should always be preceded by an empty line. The comment should be at the same indentation level as the following line.

- As a trailing comment at the end of a line of code. There should be at least one indent level between the code and the comment. The comment should not go beyond the maximum line length. If it does, then move the comment above the line of code.

- To comment out large portions of code (many editors automatically comment out multiple lines).

Single-line comments should not be used on consecutive lines unless you're commenting out large portions of code. Multiline comments should be used when long comment text is required.

Here are some examples:

```
// Good
if (condition) {

    // if you made it here, then all security checks passed
    allowed();
}

// Bad: No empty line preceding comment
if (condition) {
    // if you made it here, then all security checks passed
    allowed();
}

// Bad: Wrong indentation
if (condition) {

// if you made it here, then all security checks passed
    allowed();
}

// Good
var result = something + somethingElse;    // somethingElse will never be null

// Bad: Not enough space between code and comment
var result = something + somethingElse;// somethingElse will never be null

// Good
// if (condition) {
//     doSomething();
//     thenDoSomethingElse();
// }

// Bad: This should be a multiline comment
// This next piece of code is quite difficult, so let me explain.
// What you want to do is determine whether the condition is true
// and only then allow the user in. The condition is calculated
// from several different functions and may change during the
// lifetime of the session.
if (condition) {
    // if you made it here, then all security checks passed
    allowed();
}
```

Multiline Comments

Multiline comments are capable of spanning multiple lines. They begin with /* and end with */. Multiline comments aren't required to span multiple lines; that choice is up to you. The following are all valid multiline comments:

```
/* My comment */

/* Another comment.
This one goes to two lines. */

/*
Yet another comment.
Also goes to a second line.
*/
```

Although all of these comments are technically valid, I prefer the Java-style multiline comment pattern. The Java style is to have at least three lines: one for the /*, one or more lines beginning with a * that is aligned with the * on the previous line, and the last line for */. The resulting comment looks like this:

```
/*
 * Yet another comment.
 * Also goes to a second line.
 */
```

The result is a more legible comment that is visually aligned on the left to an asterisk. IDEs such as NetBeans and Eclipse will automatically insert these leading asterisks for you.

Multiline comments always come immediately before the code that they describe. As with single-line comments, multiline comments should be preceded by an empty line and should be at the same indentation level as the code being described. Here are some examples:

```
// Good
if (condition) {

    /*
     * if you made it here,
     * then all security checks passed
     */
    allowed();
}

// Bad: No empty line preceding comment
if (condition) {
    /*
     * if you made it here,
     * then all security checks passed
     */
    allowed();
}
```

```
// Bad: Missing a space after asterisk
if (condition) {

    /*
     *if you made it here,
     *then all security checks passed
     */
    allowed();
}

// Bad: Wrong indentation
if (condition) {

/*
 * if you made it here,
 * then all security checks passed
 */
    allowed();
}

// Bad: Don't use multiline comments for trailing comments
var result = something + somethingElse;    /*somethingElse will never be null*/
```

Using Comments

When to comment is a topic that always fosters great debate among developers. The general guidance is to comment when something is unclear and not to comment when something is apparent from the code itself. For example, the comment in this example doesn't add any understanding to the code:

```
// Bad

// Initialize count
var count = 10;
```

It's apparent from just the code that count is being initialized. The comment adds no value whatsoever. If, on the other hand, the value 10 has some special meaning that you couldn't possibly know from looking at the code, then a comment would be very useful:

```
// Good

// Changing this value will make it rain frogs
var count = 10;
```

As implausible as it may be to make it rain frogs by changing the value of count, this is an example of a good comment, because it tells you something that you otherwise would be unaware of. Imagine how confused you would be if you changed the value and it started to rain frogs...all because a comment was missing.

So the general rule is to add comments where they clarify the code.

Difficult-to-Understand Code

Difficult-to-understand code should always be commented. Depending on what the code is doing, you may use one multiline comment, several single comments, or some combination thereof. They key is to bring some understanding of the code's purpose to someone else. For example, here's some code from the YUI library's `Y.mix()` method:

```
// Good

if (mode) {

    /*
     * In mode 2 (prototype to prototype and object to object), we recurse
     * once to do the proto to proto mix. The object to object mix will be
     * handled later on.
     */
    if (mode === 2) {
        Y.mix(receiver.prototype, supplier.prototype, overwrite,
                whitelist, 0, merge);
    }

    /*
     * Depending on which mode is specified, we may be copying from or to
     * the prototypes of the supplier and receiver.
     */
    from = mode === 1 || mode === 3 ? supplier.prototype : supplier;
    to   = mode === 1 || mode === 4 ? receiver.prototype : receiver;

    /*
     * If either the supplier or receiver doesn't actually have a
     * prototype property, then we could end up with an undefined from
     * or to. If that happens, we abort and return the receiver.
     */
    if (!from || !to) {
        return receiver;
    }
} else {
    from = supplier;
    to   = receiver;
}
```

The `Y.mix()` method uses constants to determine how to proceed. The `mode` argument is equivalent to one of those constants, but it's hard to understand what each constant means just from the numeric value. The code is commented well, because it explains what otherwise appear to be complex decisions.

Potential Author Errors

Another good time to comment code is when the code appears to have an error. Teams often get bitten by well-meaning developers who find some code that looks problematic, so they fix it. Except that the code wasn't the source of a problem, so "fixing" it actually creates a problem that needs to be tracked down. Whenever you're writing code that could appear incorrect to another developer, make sure to include a comment. Here's another example from YUI:

```
while (element &&(element = element[axis])) { // NOTE: assignment
    if ( (all || element[TAG_NAME]) &&
       (!fn || fn(element)) ) {
            return element;
    }
}
```

In this case, the developer used an assignment operator in the `while` loop control condition. This isn't standard practice and will typically be flagged by linting tools as a problem. If you were unfamiliar with this code and came across this line without a comment, it would be easy to assume that this was an error, and the author meant to use the equality operator == instead of the assignment operator =. The trailing comment on that line indicates the use of the assignment operator is intentional. Now any other developer who comes along and reads the code won't be likely to make a bad "fix."

Browser-Specific Hacks

JavaScript developers are often forced to use code that is inefficient, inelegant, or downright dirty to get older browsers to work correctly. This behavior is actually a special type of potential author error: code that isn't obviously doing something browser-specific may appear to be an error. Here's an example from the YUI library's `Y.DOM.contains()` method:

```
var ret = false;

if ( !needle || !element || !needle[NODE_TYPE] || !element[NODE_TYPE]) {
    ret = false;
} else if (element[CONTAINS])  {
    // IE & SAF contains fail if needle not an ELEMENT_NODE
    if (Y.UA.opera || needle[NODE_TYPE] === 1) {
        ret = element[CONTAINS](needle);
    } else {
        ret = Y_DOM._bruteContains(element, needle);
    }
} else if (element[COMPARE_DOCUMENT_POSITION]) { // gecko
    if (element === needle || !!(element[COMPARE_DOCUMENT_POSITION](needle) & 16)) {
        ret = true;
    }
}

return ret;
```

Line 6 of this code has a very important comment. Even though Internet Explorer and Safari both include the `contains()` method natively, the method will fail if `needle` is not an element. So the method should be used only if the browser is Opera or `needle` is an element (`nodeType` is 1). The note about the browsers, and also why the `if` statement is needed, not only ensures that no one will change it unexpectedly in the future, but allows the author to revisit this code later and realize that it may be time to verify whether newer versions of Internet Explorer and Safari show the same issue.

Documentation Comments

Documentation comments aren't technically part of JavaScript, but they are a very common practice. Document comments may take many forms, but the most popular is the form that matches JavaDoc documentation format: a multiline comment with an extra asterisk at the beginning (/**) followed by a description, followed by one or more attributes indicated by the @ sign. Here's an example from YUI:

```
/**
Returns a new object containing all of the properties of all the supplied
objects. The properties from later objects will overwrite those in earlier
objects.

Passing in a single object will create a shallow copy of it. For a deep copy,
use `clone()`.

@method merge
@param {Object} objects* One or more objects to merge.
@return {Object} A new merged object.
**/
Y.merge = function () {
    var args   = arguments,
        i      = 0,
        len    = args.length,
        result = {};

    for (; i < len; ++i) {
        Y.mix(result, args[i], true);
    }

    return result;
};
```

The YUI library uses its own tool called YUIDoc to generate documentation from these comments. However, the format is almost exactly the same as the library-agnostic JSDoc Toolkit, which is widely used on open source projects as well as within Google. The key difference between YUIDoc and JSDoc Toolkit is that YUIDoc supports both HTML and Markdown in documentation comments, whereas JSDoc Toolkit supports only HTML.

It is highly recommended that you use a documentation generator with your JavaScript. The format of the comments must match the tool that you use, but the JavaDoc-style documentation comments are well supported across many documentation generators. When using documentation comments, you should be sure to document the following:

All methods

Be sure to include a description of the method, expected arguments, and possible return values.

All constructors

Comments should include the purpose of the custom type and expected arguments.

All objects with documented methods

If an object has one or more methods with documentation comments, then it also must be documented for proper documentation generation.

Of course, the exact comment format and how comments should be used will ultimately be determined by the documentation generator you choose.

CHAPTER 3

Statements and Expressions

Statements such as `if` and `for` can be used in two ways in JavaScript, with curly braces for multiple contained lines or without curly braces for one contained line. For example:

```
// Bad, though technically valid JavaScript
if(condition)
    doSomething();

// Bad, though technically valid JavaScript
if(condition) doSomething();

// Good
if (condition) {
    doSomething();
}

// Bad, though technically valid JavaScript
if (condition) { doSomething(); }
```

The first two forms, which use an `if` statement without braces, are explicitly disallowed in Crockford's Code Conventions, the jQuery Core Style Guide, the SproutCore Style Guide, and the Dojo Style Guide. The omission of braces also generates warnings by default in both JSLint and JSHint.

An overwhelming majority of JavaScript developers are in agreement that block statements should always use braces and always occupy multiple lines instead of one. This is because of the confusion created when braces aren't included. Consider the following:

```
if (condition)
    doSomething();
    doSomethingElse();
```

It's difficult to tell the author's intent in this code. There's clearly an error here, but it's impossible to know whether the error is an indentation error (the last line should not be indented) or braces are missing because both line 2 and line 3 need to be executed inside the `if` statement. Adding braces makes the error easier to find. Here are two other examples with errors:

```
if (condition) {
    doSomething();
}
    doSomethingElse();

if (condition) {
    doSomething();
doSomethingElse();
}
```

In both of these examples, the code error is clear, as both obviously have indentation errors. The braces allow you to very quickly determine the author's intent and make an appropriate change without fear of changing the code logic.

Braces should be used for all block statements, including:

- `if`
- `for`
- `while`
- `do...while`
- `try...catch...finally`

Brace Alignment

A second topic related to block statements is the alignment of braces. There are two main styles of brace alignment. The first is to have the opening brace on the same line as the beginning of the block statement, as in this example:

```
if (condition) {
    doSomething();
} else {
    doSomethingElse();
}
```

JavaScript inherited this style from Java, where it is documented in the Code Conventions for the Java Programming Language. This style also now appears in Crockford's Code Conventions, the jQuery Core Style Guide, the SproutCore Style Guide, the Google JavaScript Style Guide, and the Dojo Style Guide.

The second style of brace alignment places the opening brace on the line following the beginning of the block statement, as in this example:

```
if (condition)
{
    doSomething();
}
else
{
    doSomethingElse();
}
```

This style was made popular by C#, as Visual Studio enforces this alignment. There are no major JavaScript guides that recommend this style, and the Google JavaScript Style Guide explicitly forbids it due to fears of automatic semicolon insertion errors. My recommendation is to use the previous brace alignment format.

Block Statement Spacing

Spacing around the first line of a block statement is also a matter of preference. There are three primary styles for block statement spacing. The first is to have no spaces separating the statement name, the opening parenthesis, and the opening brace:

```
if(condition){
    doSomething();
}
```

This style is preferred by some programmers because it is more compact, though some complain that the compactness actually inhibits legibility. The Dojo Style Guide recommends this style.

The second style is to have a space separation before the opening parenthesis and after the closing parenthesis, such as:

```
if (condition) {
    doSomething();
}
```

Some programmers prefer this style because it makes the statement type and condition more legible. This is the style recommended by Crockford's Code Conventions and the Google JavaScript Style Guide.

The third style adds spaces after the opening parenthesis and before the closing parenthesis, as in the following:

```
if ( condition ) {
    doSomething();
}
```

This is the style prescribed in the jQuery Core Style Guide, because it makes all aspects of the statement start quite clear and legible.

I prefer the second style as a nice compromise between the first and third styles.

The switch Statement

Developers tend to have a love-hate relationship with the switch statement. There are varying ideas about how to use switch statements and how to format them. Some of this variance comes from the switch statement's lineage, originating in C and making its way through Java into JavaScript without the exact same syntax.

Despite the similar syntax, JavaScript `switch` statements behave differently than in other languages: any type of value may be used in a `switch` statement, and any expression can be used as a valid `case`. Other languages require the use of primitive values and constants, respectively.

Indentation

Indentation of the `switch` statement is a matter of debate among JavaScript developers. Many use the Java style of formatting `switch` statements, which looks like this:

```
switch(condition) {
    case "first":
        // code
        break;

    case "second":
        // code
        break;

    case "third":
        // code
        break;

    default:
        // code
}
```

The unique parts of this format are:

- Each `case` statement is indented one level from the `switch` keyword.
- There is an extra line before and after each `case` statement from the second one on.

The format of `switch` statements is rarely included in style guides when this style is used, primarily because it is the format that many editors use automatically.

Although this is the format that I prefer, both Crockford's Code Conventions and the Dojo Style Guide recommend a slightly different format:

```
switch(condition) {
case "first":
    // code
    break;
case "second":
    // code
    break;
case "third":
    // code
    break;
default:
    // code
}
```

The major difference between this and the previous format is that the `case` keyword is aligned to the same column as the `switch` keyword. Note also that there are no blank lines in between any parts of the statement. JSLint expects this indentation format for `switch` statements by default and will warn if a `case` is not aligned with `switch`. This option may also be turned on and off via the "Tolerate messy white space" option. JSLint does not warn if additional blank lines are included.

As with other aspects of coding style, this choice is completely a matter of preference.

Falling Through

Another popular source of debate is whether falling through from one `case` to another is an acceptable practice. Accidentally omitting a `break` at the end of a `case` is a very common source of bugs, so Douglas Crockford argues that every `case` should end with `break`, `return`, or `throw`, without exception. JSLint warns when one `case` falls through into another.

I agree with those who consider falling through to be an acceptable method of programming, as long as it is clearly indicated, such as:

```
switch(condition) {

    // obvious fall through
    case "first":
    case "second":
        // code
        break;

    case "third":
        // code

        /*falls through*/
    default:
        // code
}
```

This `switch` statement has two obvious fall-throughs. The first `case` falls through into the second, which is considered an acceptable practice (even by JSLint) because there are no statements to run for just the first `case` and there are no extra lines separating the two `case` statements.

The second instance is with `case "third"`, which falls through into the `default` handler. This fall-through is marked with a comment to indicate developer intent. In this code, it's obvious that the `case` is meant to fall through and isn't a mistake. JSHint typically warns when a `case` falls through unless you include this comment, in which case the warning is turned off because you've signaled that this isn't an error.

Crockford's Code Conventions disallows fall-throughs in `switch` statements altogether. The jQuery Core Style Guide mentions that fall-throughs are used in their code, and the Dojo Style Guide gives an example with a fall-through comment. My recommendation is to allow fall-throughs as long as a comment is used to indicate that the fall-through is intentional.

default

Another point of contention with regard to `switch` is whether a `default` case is required. Some believe that a `default` should always be included even if the default action is to do nothing, as in:

```
switch(condition) {
    case "first":
        // code
        break;

    case "second":
        // code
        break;

    default:
        // do nothing
}
```

You're likely to find open source JavaScript code following this pattern, including `default` and just leaving a comment that nothing should happen there. Although no style guides are explicit about this, both Douglas Crockford's Code Conventions for the JavaScript Programming Language and the Dojo Style Guide include `default` as part of their standard `switch` statement format.

My preference is to omit `default` when there is no default action and annotate it using a comment, as in this example:

```
switch(condition) {
    case "first":
        // code
        break;

    case "second":
        // code
        break;

    // no default
}
```

This way, the code author's intent is clear that there should be no default action, and you save some bytes by not including extra unnecessary syntax.

The with Statement

The with statement changes how the containing context interprets variables. It allows properties and methods from a particular object to be accessed as if they were local variables and functions, omitting the object identifier altogether. The intent of with was to lessen the amount of typing developers need to do when using multiple object members in close proximity. For example:

```
var book = {
    title: "Maintainable JavaScript",
    author: "Nicholas C. Zakas"
};

var message = "The book is ";

with (book) {
    message += title;
    message += " by " + author;
}
```

In this code, the with statement is used to augment identifier resolution within the curly braces by allowing the properties of book to be accessed as if they were variables. The problem is that it's hard to tell where title and author originated from. It's not clear that these are properties of book and that message is a local variable. This confusion actually extends far beyond developers, with JavaScript engines and minifiers being forced to skip optimization of this section for fear of guessing incorrectly.

The with statement is actually disallowed in strict mode, causing a syntax error and indicating the ECMAScript committee's belief that with should no longer be used. Crockford's Code Conventions and the Google JavaScript Style Guide disallow the use of with. I strongly recommend avoiding the with statement, as it prevents you from easily applying strict mode to your code (a practice I recommend).

The for Loop

There are two types of for loops: the traditional for loop that JavaScript inherited from C and Java, as well as the for-in loop that iterates over properties for an object. These two loops, though similar, have two very different uses. The traditional for loop is typically used to iterate over members of an array, such as:

```
var values = [ 1, 2, 3, 4, 5, 6, 7 ],
    i, len;

for (i=0, len=values.length; i < len; i++) {
    process(values[i]);
}
```

There are two ways to modify how the loop proceeds (aside from using a return or throw statement). The first is to use the break statement. Using break causes the loop to exit immediately and not continue running even if the loop hasn't finished all iterations. For example:

```
var values = [ 1, 2, 3, 4, 5, 6, 7 ],
    i, len;

for (i=0, len=values.length; i < len; i++) {
    if (i == 2) {
        break;  // no more iterations
    }
    process(values[i]);
}
```

The body of this loop will execute two times and then exit before executing process() the third time, even if the values array has more than three items.

The second way to modify how a loop proceeds is through the use of continue. The continue statement exits the loop immediately; however, the loop will continue with the next iteration. Here's an example:

```
var values = [ 1, 2, 3, 4, 5, 6, 7 ],
    i, len;

for (i=0, len=values.length; i < len; i++) {
    if (i == 2) {
        continue;   // skip just this iteration
    }
    process(values[i]);
}
```

The body of this loop executes two times, skips the third time, and picks up with the fourth iteration. The loop will then continue until its last iteration unless otherwise interfered with.

Crockford's Code Conventions disallows the use of continue. His assertion is that code using continue can better be written using conditions. For instance, the previous example can be rewritten as:

```
var values = [ 1, 2, 3, 4, 5, 6, 7 ],
    i, len;

for (i=0, len=values.length; i < len; i++) {
    if (i != 2) {
        process(values[i]);
    }
}
```

Crockford argues that this pattern is easier for developers to understand and less error prone. The Dojo Style Guide states explicitly that continue, along with break, may be used. My recommendation is to avoid continue whenever possible, but there is no reason to completely forbid it. The readability of the code should dictate its usage.

JSLint warns when continue is used. JSHint does not warn when continue is used.

The for-in Loop

The `for-in` loop is used to iterate over properties of an object. Instead of defining a control condition, the loop systematically goes through each named object property and returns the property name inside of a variable, as in:

```
var prop;

for (prop in object) {
    console.log("Property name is " + prop);
    console.log("Property value is " + object[prop]);
}
```

A problem with `for-in` is that it returns not only instance properties of an object but also all properties it inherits through the prototype. You may thus end up with unanticipated results when iterating through properties on your own object. For this reason, it's best to filter the `for-in` loop to only instance properties by using `hasOwnProperty()`. Here's an example:

```
var prop;

for (prop in object) {
    if (object.hasOwnProperty(prop)) {
        console.log("Property name is " + prop);
        console.log("Property value is " + object[prop]);
    }
}
```

Crockford's Code Conventions require the use of `hasOwnProperty()` for all `for-in` loops. Both JSLint and JSHint warn when a `for-in` loop is missing a call to `hasOwnProperty()` by default (both allow this option to be turned off). My recommendation is to always use `hasOwnProperty()` for `for-in` loops unless you're intentionally looking up the prototype chain, in which case it should be indicated with a comment, such as:

```
var prop;

for (prop in object) {    // include prototype properties
    console.log("Property name is " + prop);
    console.log("Property value is " + object[prop]);
}
```

Another area of focus with `for-in` loops is their usage with objects. A common mistake is to use `for-in` to iterate over members of an array, as in this example:

```
// Bad
var values = [ 1, 2, 3, 4, 5, 6, 7],
    i;

for (i in values) {
    process(items[i]);
}
```

This practice is disallowed in Crockford's Code Conventions as well as the Google JavaScript Style Guide due to the potential errors it may cause. Remember, the `for-in` is iterating over object keys on both the instance and the prototype, so it's not limited to the numerically indexed properties of the array. The `for-in` loop should never be used in this way.

CHAPTER 4

Variables, Functions, and Operators

The real guts of any JavaScript program are the functions you write to accomplish tasks. Inside the functions, variables and operators are used to move bits around and make things happen. That's why, after getting the basic formatting of your JavaScript down, it's important to decide how to use functions, variables, and operators to reduce complexity and improve readability.

Variable Declarations

Variable declarations are accomplished by using the var statement. JavaScript allows the var statement to be used multiple times and nearly anywhere within a script. This usage creates interesting cognitive issues for developers, because all var statements are hoisted to the top of the containing function regardless of where they actually occur in the code. For example:

```
function doSomething() {

    var result = 10 + value;
    var value = 10;
    return result;
}
```

In this code, it's perfectly valid for the variable value to be used before it was declared, though it will cause result to have the special value NaN. To understand why, you need to be aware that this code is changed by the JavaScript engine to this:

```
function doSomething() {

    var result;
    var value;

    result = 10 + value;
    value = 10;

    return result;
}
```

The two var statements are hoisted to the top of the function; the initialization happens afterward. The variable value has the special value undefined when it's used on line 6, so result becomes NaN (not a number). Only after that is value finally assigned the value of 10.

One area where developers tend to miss variable declaration hoisting is with for statements, in which variables are declared as part of the initialization:

```
function doSomethingWithItems(items) {

    for (var i=0, len=items.length; i < len; i++) {
        doSomething(items[i]);
    }
}
```

JavaScript up to ECMAScript 5 has no concept of block-level variable declarations, so this code is actually equivalent to the following:

```
function doSomethingWithItems(items) {

    var i, len;

    for (i=0, len=items.length; i < len; i++) {
        doSomething(items[i]);
    }
}
```

Variable declaration hoisting means defining a variable anywhere in a function is the same as declaring it at the top of the function. Therefore, a popular style is to have all variables declared at the top of a function instead of scattered throughout. In short, you end up writing code similar to the manner in which the JavaScript engine will interpret it.

My recommendation is to have your local variables defined as the first statements in a function. This approach is recommended in Crockford's Code Conventions, the SproutCore Style Guide, and the Dojo Style Guide:

```
function doSomethingWithItems(items) {

    var i, len;
    var value = 10;
    var result = value + 10;

    for (i=0, len=items.length; i < len; i++) {
        doSomething(items[i]);
    }
}
```

Crockford goes on to recommend the use of a single var statement at the top of functions:

```
function doSomethingWithItems(items) {

    var i, len,
        value = 10,
        result = value + 10;

    for (i=0, len=items.length; i < len; i++) {
        doSomething(items[i]);
    }
}
```

The Dojo Style Guide allows combining **var** statements only when the variables are related to one another.

My personal preference is to combine all **var** statements with one initialized variable per line. The equals signs should be aligned. For variables that aren't initialized, they should appear last, as in the following example:

```
function doSomethingWithItems(items) {

    var value   = 10,
        result  = value + 10,
        i,
        len;

    for (i=0, len=items.length; i < len; i++) {
        doSomething(items[i]);
    }
}
```

At a minimum, I recommend combining **var** statements, as doing so makes your code smaller and therefore faster to download.

Function Declarations

Function declarations, just like variable declarations, are hoisted by JavaScript engines. Therefore, it's possible to use a function in code before it is declared:

```
// Bad
doSomething();

function doSomething() {
    alert("Hello world!");
}
```

This approach works because the JavaScript engine interprets the code as if it were the following:

```
function doSomething() {
    alert("Hello world!");
}

doSomething();
```

Due to this behavior, it's recommended that JavaScript functions always be declared before being used. This design appears in Crockford's Code Conventions. Crockford also recommends that local functions be placed immediately after variable declarations within a containing function, as in:

```
function doSomethingWithItems(items) {

    var i, len,
        value = 10,
        result = value + 10;

    function doSomething(item) {
        // do something
    }

    for (i=0, len=items.length; i < len; i++) {
        doSomething(items[i]);
    }
}
```

Both JSLint and JSHint will warn when a function is used before it is declared.

Additionally, function declarations should never appear inside of block statements. For example, this code won't behave as expected:

```
// Bad
if (condition) {
    function doSomething() {
        alert("Hi!");
    }
} else {
    function doSomething() {
        alert("Yo!");
    }
}
```

Exactly how this will work from browser to browser will vary. Most browsers automatically take the second declaration without evaluating `condition`; Firefox evaluates `condition` and uses the appropriate function declaration. This is a gray area in the ECMAScript specification and should thus be avoided. Function declarations should be used only outside of conditional statements. This pattern is explicitly forbidden in the Google JavaScript Style Guide.

Function Call Spacing

Almost universally, the recommended style for function calls is to have no space between the function name and the opening parenthesis, which is done to differentiate it from a block statement. For example:

```
// Good
doSomething(item);
```

```
// Bad: Looks like a block statement
doSomething (item);

// Block statement for comparison
while (item) {
    // do something
}
```

Crockford's Code Conventions explicitly calls this out. The Dojo Style Guide, Sprout-Core Style Guide, and Google JavaScript Style Guide implicitly recommend this style through code examples.

The jQuery Core Style Guide further specifies that an extra space should be included after the opening parenthesis and before the closing parenthesis, such as:

```
// jQuery-style
doSomething( item );
```

The intent here is to make the arguments easier to read. The jQuery Core Style Guide also lists some exceptions to this style, specifically relating to functions that are passed a single argument that is an object literal, array literal, function expression, or string. So the following examples are all still considered valid:

```
// jQuery exceptions
doSomething(function() {});
doSomething({ item: item });
doSomething([ item ]);
doSomething("Hi!");
```

Generally speaking, styles with more than one exception are not good, because they can be confusing to developers.

Immediate Function Invocation

JavaScript allows you to declare anonymous functions—functions without proper names—and assign those functions to variables or properties. For example:

```
var doSomething = function() {
    // function body
};
```

Such anonymous functions can also be immediately invoked to return a value to the variable by including parentheses at the very end:

```
// Bad
var value = function() {

    // function body

    return {
        message: "Hi"
    }
}();
```

In the previous example, `value` ends up being assigned an object, because the function is immediately invoked. The problem with this pattern is that it looks very similar to assigning an anonymous function to a variable. You don't know that this isn't the case until you get to the very last line and see the parentheses. This sort of confusion hinders the readability of your code.

To make it obvious that immediate function invocation is taking place, put parentheses around the function, as in this example:

```
// Good
var value = (function() {

    // function body

    return {
        message: "Hi"
    }
}());
```

This code now has a signal on the first line, the open paren, that the function is immediately invoked. Adding the parentheses doesn't change the behavior of the code at all. Crockford's Code Conventions recommends this pattern, and JSLint will warn when the parentheses are missing.

Strict Mode

ECMAScript 5 introduced *strict mode*, a way to alter how JavaScript is executed and parsed in the hopes of reducing errors. To put a script into strict mode, use the following pragma:

```
"use strict";
```

Although this looks like a string that isn't assigned to a variable, ECMAScript 5 JavaScript engines treat this as a command to switch into strict mode. This pragma is valid both globally as well as locally, inside of a single function. However, it's a common recommendation (though undocumented in any popular style guide) to avoid placing `"use strict"` in the global scope. The reason is that strict mode applies to all code in a single file, so if you're concatenating 11 files and one of them has global strict mode enabled, all of the files are placed into strict mode. Because strict mode operates under slightly different rules than nonstrict mode, there's a high likelihood of errors within the other files. For this reason, it's best to avoid placing `"use strict"` in the global scope. Here are some examples:

```
// Bad - global strict mode
"use strict";

function doSomething() {
    // code
}
```

```
// Good
function doSomething() {
    "use strict";

    // code
}
```

If you want strict mode to apply to multiple functions without needing to write "use strict" multiple times, use immediate function invocation:

```
// Good
(function() {
    "use strict";

    function doSomething() {
        // code
    }

    function doSomethingElse() {
        // code
    }

})();
```

In this example, doSomething() and doSomethingElse() both run in strict mode, because they are contained in an immediately invoked function with "use strict" specified.

Both JSLint and JSHint warn when "use strict" is found outside of a function. Both also expect all functions to have "use strict" specified by default; this can be turned off in both tools. I recommend using strict mode wherever possible to limit common mistakes.

Equality

Equality in JavaScript is tricky due to *type coercion*. Type coercion causes variables of a specific type to be converted automatically into a different type for a particular operation to succeed, which can lead to some unexpected results.

One of the main areas in which type coercion occurs is with the use of equality operators, == and !=. These two operators cause type coercion when the two values being compared are not the same data type (when they are the same data type, no coercion occurs). There are many instances in which code may not be doing what you expect.

If you compare a number to a string, the string is first converted to a number, and then the comparison happens. Some examples:

```
// The number 5 and string 5
console.log(5 == "5");          // true

// The number 25 and hexadecimal string 25
console.log(25 == "0x19");      // true
```

When performing type coercion, the string is converted to a number as if using the `Number()` casting function. Because `Number()` understands hexadecimal format, it will convert a string that looks like a hexadecimal number into the decimal equivalent before the comparison occurs.

If a boolean value is compared to a number, then the boolean is converted to a number before comparison. A `false` value becomes 0 and `true` becomes 1. For example:

```
// The number 1 and true
console.log(1 == true);     // true

// The number 0 and false
console.log(0 == false);    // true

// The number 2 and true
console.log(2 == true);     // false
```

If one of the values is an object and the other is not, then the object's `valueOf()` method is called to get a primitive value to compare against. If `valueOf()` is not defined, then `toString()` is called instead. After that point, the comparison continues following the previously discussed rules about mixed type comparisons. For example:

```
var object = {
    toString: function() {
        return "0x19";
    }
};

console.log(object == 25);      // true
```

The object is deemed to be equal to the number 25 because its `toString()` method returned the hexadecimal string `"0x19"`, which was then converted to a number before being compared to 25.

The last instance of type coercion occurs between `null` and `undefined`. These two special values are deemed to be equivalent simply by the letter of the ECMAScript standard:

```
console.log(null == undefined);     // true
```

Because of type coercion, avoiding == and != at all is recommended; instead, use === and !==. These operators perform comparison without type coercion. So if two values don't have the same data type, they are automatically considered to be unequal, which allows your comparison statements to always perform the comparison in a way that is more consistent. Consider the differences between == and === in a few cases:

```
// The number 5 and string 5
console.log(5 == "5");          // true
console.log(5 === "5");         // false

// The number 25 and hexadecimal string 25
console.log(25 == "0x19");      // true
console.log(25 === "0x19");     // false
```

```
// The number 1 and true
console.log(1 == true);       // true
console.log(1 === true);      // false

// The number 0 and false
console.log(0 == false);      // true
console.log(0 === false);     // false

// The number 2 and true
console.log(2 == true);       // false
console.log(2 === true);      // false

var object = {
    toString: function() {
        return "0x19";
    }
};

// An object and 25
console.log(object == 25);    // true
console.log(object === 25);   // false

// Null and undefined
console.log(null == undefined); // true
console.log(null === undefined);// false
```

Use of === and !== is recommended by Crockford's Code Conventions, the jQuery Core Style Guide, and the SproutCore Style Guide. Crockford's guide recommends usage all the time, but specifically for comparing against false values (those values that are co-erced to false, such as 0, the empty string, null, and undefined). The jQuery Core Style Guide allows the use of == for comparison against null when the intent is to test for both null and undefined. I recommend using === and !== all the time without exception.

JSLint warns about all uses of == and != by default. JSHint warns about using == and != when comparing to a false value by default. You can enable warnings for all uses of == and != by adding the eqeqeq option.

eval()

The eval() function takes a string of JavaScript code and executes it. This function allows developers to download additional JavaScript code, or to generate JavaScript code on the fly, and then execute it. For example:

```
eval("alert('Hi!')");

var count = 10;
var number = eval("5 + count");
console.log(number);     // 15
```

The `eval()` function isn't the only way to execute a JavaScript string from within Java-Script. The same can be done using the `Function` constructor as well as `setTimeout()` and `setInterval()`. Here are some examples:

```
var myfunc = new Function("alert('Hi!')");

setTimeout("document.body.style.background='red'", 50);

setInterval("document.title = 'It is now '" + (new Date()), 1000);
```

All of these are considered bad practice by most of the JavaScript community. Although `eval()` may be used from time to time in JavaScript libraries (mostly in relation to JSON), the other three uses are rarely, if ever, used. A good general guideline is to never use `Function` and to use `eval()` only if no other options are present. Both `setTime out()` and `setInterval()` can be used but should use function instead of strings:

```
setTimeout(function() {
    document.body.style.background='red';
}, 50);

setInterval(function() {
    document.title = 'It is now ' + (new Date());
}, 1000);
```

Crockford's Code Conventions forbids the use of `eval()` and `Function`, as well as `set Timeout()` and `setInterval()` when used with strings. The jQuery Core Style Guide forbids the use of `eval()` except for a JSON parsing fallback used in one place. The Google JavaScript Style Guide allows the use of `eval()` only for converting Ajax responses into JavaScript values.

Both JSLint and JSHint warn about the use of `eval()`, `Function`, `setTimeout()`, and `setInterval()` by default.

> ECMAScript 5 strict mode puts severe restrictions on `eval()`, preventing it from creating new variables or functions in the enclosing scope. This restriction helps close some of the security holes innate in `eval()`. However, avoiding `eval()` is still recommended unless there is absolutely no other way to accomplish the task.

Primitive Wrapper Types

A little-known and often misunderstood aspect of JavaScript is the language's reliance on primitive wrapper types. There are three primitive wrapper types: `String`, `Boolean`, and `Number`. Each of these types exists as a constructor in the global scope and each represents the object form of its respective primitive type. The main use of primitive wrapper types is to make primitive values act like objects, for instance:

```
var name = "Nicholas";
console.log(name.toUpperCase());
```

Even though `name` is a string, which is a primitive type and therefore not an object, you're still able to use methods such as `toUpperCase()` as if the string were an object. This usage is made possible because the JavaScript engine creates a new instance of the `String` type behind the scenes for just that statement. Afterward, it's destroyed, and another is created when it is needed. You can test out this behavior by trying to add a property to a string:

```
var name = "Nicholas";
name.author = true;
console.log(name.author);    // undefined
```

The `author` property has vanished after the second line. That's because the temporary `String` object representing the string was destroyed after line 2 executed, and a new `String` object was created for line 3. It's possible to create these objects yourself as well:

```
// Bad
var name = new String("Nicholas");
var author = new Boolean(true);
var count = new Number(10);
```

Although it's possible to use these primitive wrapper types, I strongly recommend avoiding them. Developers tend to get confused as to whether they're dealing with an object or a primitive, and bugs occur. There isn't any reason to create these objects yourself.

The Google JavaScript Style Guide forbids the use of primitive wrapper types. Both JSLint and JSHint will warn if you try to use `String`, `Number`, or `Boolean` to create new objects.

PART II

Programming Practices

"There are two ways of constructing a software design: One way is to make it so simple that there are obviously no deficiencies and the other way is to make it so complicated that there are no obvious deficiencies." —C.A.R. Hoare, The 1980 ACM Turing Award Lecture

The first part of this book covered style guidelines for JavaScript. Style guidelines are aimed at making code look the same regardless of who is working on it. What style guidelines don't cover is how to solve common problems. That's where programming practices come in.

Programming practices are another type of code convention. Whereas style guidelines are concerned with the appearance of code, programming practices are concerned with the outcome of the code. You can think of programming practices like recipes—they help developers write their code in such a way that the end result is already known. If you've ever used design patterns such as the observer pattern of the model-view-controller (MVC), then you're already familiar with programming practices. Design patterns are programming practices that solve specific problems related to software organization.

The programming practices in this section cover very small problems. These practices may be considered design patterns by some, but most are simple tips for improving the overall quality of your code.

Both JSLint and JSHint include some warnings for programming practices in addition to stylistic issues. It is highly recommended that you use one of these tools in your JavaScript development to ensure that small and hard-to-find issues are flagged.

CHAPTER 5

Loose Coupling of UI Layers

In web development, the user interface (UI) is defined by three separate layers working together:

- HTML is used to define the data and semantics of the page.
- CSS is used to style the page, creating visual distinction.
- JavaScript is used to add behavior to the page, making it more interactive.

These UI layers are usually pictured as HTML being at the base, with CSS and JavaScript layers on top, as displayed in Figure 5-1.

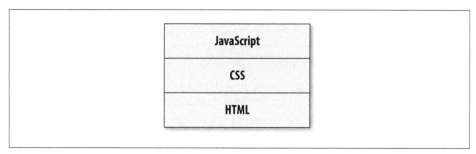

Figure 5-1. The layers of a web user interface

In reality, though, CSS and JavaScript are more like siblings rather than JavaScript having a dependency on CSS. It's possible to have a page with just HTML and CSS without any JavaScript, and it's possible to have a page with just HTML and JavaScript without any CSS. I prefer to think of the relationship between these three layers as displayed in Figure 5-2.

Thinking of CSS and JavaScript being of the same stature in an overall web user interface allows for more possibilities and eliminates dependencies. For example, JavaScript shouldn't rely on CSS to function correctly—it should be able to function independently of the CSS, even if there is some interaction between the two.

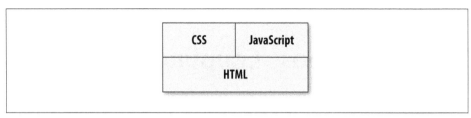

Figure 5-2. The updated layers of a web user interface

Each layer of a web UI is a piece of a larger system that must be maintained. HTML, CSS, and JavaScript are often written so tightly coupled that it's impossible to make small changes without changing one or two other layers. In a large-scale web application, this type of design is a big problem, especially on teams in which the same people aren't responsible for the HTML, CSS, and JavaScript. In such situations, loose coupling becomes very important.

What Is Loose Coupling?

Many design patterns are actually solutions to the problem of tight coupling. If two components are tightly coupled, it means that one component has direct knowledge of the other in such a way that a change to one of the components often necessitates a change to the other component. For example, suppose you have a CSS class named `error` that is used throughout a website, embedded in HTML. If one day you decide that `error` isn't the right name for the class and you want to change it to `warning`, you'll have to edit not just the CSS but also all of the HTML using that class. The HTML is tightly coupled to the CSS. This is just a simple example. Imagine what a nightmare it is when a system has dozens or hundreds of components.

Loose coupling is achieved when you're able to make changes to a single component without making changes to other components. Loose coupling is essential to the maintainability of large systems for which more than one person is responsible for the development and maintenance of code. You absolutely want developers to be able to make changes in one area of the code without breaking what other developers are doing in a different area of code.

Loose coupling is achieved by limiting each component's knowledge of the larger system. In essence, every component needs to be as dumb as possible to ensure loose coupling. The less a component knows, the better off the entire system tends to be.

One thing to keep in mind: there is no such thing as *no* coupling between components that work together. In any system, there will necessarily be some knowledge shared between components in order to do their job. That's okay. The goal is to ensure that changes in one component don't require changes in multiple places on a regular basis.

A web UI that is loosely coupled is easier to debug. Issues with text or structure are addressed by looking just at HTML. When stylistic issues arise, you know the problem and the fix will be in the CSS. Finally, if there are behavioral issues, you can go straight to the JavaScript to address the problem. This ability is a key part of a maintainable web interface.

Keep JavaScript Out of CSS

There was a feature in Internet Explorer 8 and earlier that some loved and many hated: CSS expressions. CSS expressions allow you to insert JavaScript directly into CSS, performing calculations or other functionality directly inside CSS code. For example, the following code sets the width of an element to match the width of the browser:

```
/* Bad */
.box {
    width: expression(document.body.offsetWidth + "px");
}
```

The CSS expression is enclosed in the special `expression()` function, which accepts any JavaScript code. CSS expressions are reevaluated frequently by the browser and were considered to be bad for performance, even making it into Steve Souders's book *High Performance Web Sites* as something to avoid (Rule 7: Avoid CSS Expressions).

Aside from the performance issues, having JavaScript embedded inside of CSS is a maintenance nightmare, and one with which I have firsthand experience. In 2005, I had a JavaScript bug assigned to me that had me baffled from the start. It occurred only in Internet Explorer and happened only when the browser window was resized a few times. At that point in time, the best JavaScript debugger for Internet Explorer was Visual Studio, but it failed to locate the source of the problem. I spent an entire day setting breakpoints and inserting `alert()` statements to try to figure out what was happening.

By the end of the day, I had resigned myself to my least favorite debugging method: systematic removal of code. I removed JavaScript, file by file, and tried to reproduce the issue. I quickly became frustrated and simply removed all JavaScript from the page. The bug was still happening. I look at my computer screen in disbelief. A JavaScript error without any JavaScript on the page—how is that even possible?

To this day, I'm still not sure what led me finally to look at the CSS. I wasn't even sure what I was looking for at that point. I just started at the top of the CSS and slowly scrolled down to see if anything would jump out at me. Finally, I saw the CSS expression that was the source of the problem. When I removed it, the JavaScript error went away.

This experience is what led me to the rules in this chapter. I spent an entire day looking for a JavaScript bug in JavaScript when it was actually in CSS. The actual error wasn't even difficult to solve, but tracking down the error in a part of the system in which I (reasonably) didn't expect to find it was ridiculously time consuming.

Fortunately, Internet Explorer 9 removed support for CSS expressions, but older versions of Internet Explorer are still in use around the world. Even though it's tempting to use a CSS expression to make up for some of the missing functionality in these older browsers, resist the urge and save yourself a lot of time and effort. Keep JavaScript out of your CSS.

Keep CSS Out of JavaScript

Keeping this clean separation between CSS and JavaScript can be challenging at times. These two languages work quite well together, so it is tempting to manipulate style data within JavaScript. The most popular way to script style changes is through the use of the `style` property on any DOM element. The `style` property is an object containing properties that allow you to read and change CSS properties. For instance, you can change the text color of an element to red like this:

```
// Bad
element.style.color = "red";
```

It's actually quite common to see large blocks of code using `style` to change multiple properties, such as:

```
// Bad
element.style.color = "red";
element.style.left = "10px";
element.style.top = "100px";
element.style.visibility = "visible";
```

This approach is problematic, because the style information is now located inside of JavaScript instead of CSS. When there is a style problem, you should be able to go straight to the CSS to find and resolve the issue. You wouldn't stop to consider that the style information is in JavaScript until you'd exhausted all other possibilities.

Another way developers use the `style` object is to set an entire CSS string via the `cssText` property, as in the following example:

```
// Bad
element.style.cssText = "color: red; left: 10px; top: 100px; visibility: hidden";
```

Using the `cssText` property is just a shortcut to set multiple CSS properties at once. This pattern has the same problem as setting individual properties: keeping style information inside of your JavaScript is a maintenance problem.

Keeping CSS out of JavaScript means that all style information still lives in CSS. When JavaScript needs to change the style of an element, the best way to do so is by manipulating CSS classes. For instance, to reveal a dialog box on the page, define a class in your CSS such as this:

```
.reveal {
    color: red;
    left: 10px;
    top: 100px;
    visibility: visible;
}
```

Then, in JavaScript, add the class to the element in question:

```
// Good - Native
element.className += " reveal";

// Good - HTML5
element.classList.add("reveal");

// Good - YUI
Y.one(element).addClass("reveal");

// Good - jQuery
$(element).addClass("reveal");

// Good - Dojo
dojo.addClass(element, "reveal");
```

Think of CSS class names as the communication mechanism between CSS and Java-Script. JavaScript is free to add and remove class names from elements throughout the life cycle of the page. The styles applied by the classes are defined in the CSS code. Those styles may change at any point in time in the CSS without necessitating a Java-Script update. JavaScript should not be manipulating styles directly so that it stays loosely coupled to the CSS.

> There is one instance in which using the `style` property is acceptable: when you need to position an element on the page relative to another element or the size of the page itself. This type of calculation can't be done in CSS, so it is okay to use `style.top`, `style.left`, `style.bottom`, and `style.right` to position an element correctly. The CSS class for the element should have a logical default value that is then overridden in script.

Keep JavaScript Out of HTML

One of the first things people do when they learn JavaScript is start embedding it within HTML. There are any number of ways to do this. The first is to assign event handlers by using the `on` attributes such as `onclick`:

```
<!-- Bad -->
<button onclick="doSomething()" id="action-btn">Click Me</button>
```

This is how most websites with JavaScript were coded around the year 2000. HTML was littered with `onclick` and other event handlers as attributes of elements. Although this code will work in most situations, it represents tight coupling of two UI layers (HTML and JavaScript), so there are several problems with it.

First, the `doSomething()` function must be available when the button is clicked. Those who developed websites around 2000 are quite familiar with this problem. The code for `doSomething()` may be loaded from an external file or may occur later in the HTML file. Either way, it's possible for a user to click the button before the function is available and cause a JavaScript error. The resulting error message may pop up to the user or cause the button to appear to do nothing. Either case is undesirable.

The second problem is a maintenance issue. What happens if you want to change the name of doSomething()? What happens if the button should now call a different function when clicked? In both cases, you're making changes to both the JavaScript and the HTML; this is the very essence of tightly coupled code.

Most—if not all—of your JavaScript should be contained in external files and included on the page via a <script> element. The on attributes should not be used for attaching event handlers in HTML. Instead, use JavaScript methods for adding event handlers once the external script has been loaded. For DOM Level 2–compliant browsers, you can achieve the same behavior in the previous example by using this code:

```
function doSomething() {
    // code
}

var btn = document.getElementById("action-btn");
btn.addEventListener("click", doSomething, false);
```

The advantage of this approach is that the function doSomething() is defined in the same file as the code that attatches the event handler. If the function name needs to change, there is just one file that needs editing; if the button should do something else when clicked, there is still just one place to go to make that change.

Internet Explorer 8 and earlier versions don't support addEventListener(), so you may need a function to normalize the difference:

```
function addListener(target, type, handler) {
    if (target.addEventListener) {
        target.addEventListener(type, handler, false);
    } else if (target.attachEvent) {
        target.attachEvent("on" + type, handler);
    } else {
        target["on" + type] = handler;
    }
}
```

This function is capable of adding an event handler for an element in any browser, even falling back to the DOM Level 0 approach of assigning a handler to the on property of an object (this step would be necessary only for very old browsers such as Netscape 4, but it's always good to cover your bases). This method is used as follows:

```
function doSomething() {
    // code
}

var btn = document.getElementById("action-btn");
addListener(btn, "click", doSomething);
```

If you're using a JavaScript library, you should use the library's methods for adding an event handler to an element. Here are some common examples for popular libraries:

```
// YUI
Y.one("#action-btn").on("click", doSomething);

// jQuery
$("#action-btn").on("click", doSomething);

// Dojo
var btn = dojo.byId("action-btn");
dojo.connect(btn, "click", doSomething);
```

Another way of embedding JavaScript in HTML is to use the `<script>` element with inline code:

```
<!-- Bad -->
<script>
    doSomething();
</script>
```

It's best to keep all JavaScript in external files and to keep inline JavaScript code out of your HTML. Part of the reason for this approach is to aid in debugging. When a JavaScript error occurs, your first inclination is to start digging through your JavaScript files to find the issue. If the JavaScript is located in the HTML, that's a workflow interruption. You first have to determine whether the JavaScript is in the JavaScript files (which it should be) or in the HTML. Only then can you start debugging.

This point might seem minor, especially given today's excellent web development tools, but it is actually an important piece of the maintenance puzzle. Predictability leads to faster debugging and development, and knowing (not guessing) where to start with a bug is what leads to faster resolutions and better overall code quality.

Keep HTML Out of JavaScript

Just as it's best to keep JavaScript out of HTML, it's also best to keep HTML out of JavaScript. As mentioned previously, when there is a text or structural issue to debug, you want to be able to go to the HTML to start debugging. Many times in my career I've had trouble tracking down such an issue because I was looking at the HTML when in fact the real issue was buried deep inside JavaScript.

HTML frequently ends up in JavaScript as a consequence of using the `innerHTML` property, as in:

```
// Bad
var div = document.getElementById("my-div");
div.innerHTML = "<h3>Error</h3><p>Invalid e-mail address.</p>";
```

Embedding HTML strings inside your JavaScript is a bad practice for a number of reasons. First, as mentioned previously, it complicates tracking down text and structural issues. The typical approach for debugging perceived markup issues is to first look at the DOM tree in the browser's inspector, then look at the HTML source of the page to find differences. Tracking down these issues becomes more problematic when Java-Script is doing more than simple DOM manipulation.

The second problem with this approach is maintainability. If you need to change text or markup, you want to be able to go to one place: the place where you manage HTML. This may be in PHP code, a JSP file, or even a template such as Mustache or Handlebars. Regardless of the mechanism used, you want all of your markup to be in one location so that it can be easily updated. Markup embedded within JavaScript isn't as accessible for changes, because it's unexpected. Why would you think to go into your JavaScript to make a markup change when most of the markup is located inside of a directory of template files?

It's far less error prone to edit markup than it is to edit JavaScript. By placing HTML into JavaScript, you've complicated the problem. JavaScript strings require proper escaping of quote characters, meaning that the markup needs slightly different syntax than it would in templates.

Because most web applications are quite dynamic in nature and JavaScript is often used to change the UI during the life cycle of the page, it is definitely necessary to use Java-Script to insert or otherwise manipulate markup on the page. There are several ways to accomplish this in a loosely coupled manner.

Alternative #1: Load from the Server

The first is to keep the templates remote and use an `XMLHttpRequest` object to retrieve additional markup. This approach is more convenient for single-page applications than for multiple-page applications. For instance, clicking on a link that should bring up a new dialog box might look like this:

```
function loadDialog(name, oncomplete) {

    var xhr = new XMLHttpRequest();
    xhr.open("get", "/js/dialog/" + name, true);

    xhr.onreadystatechange = function() {

        if (xhr.readyState == 4 && xhr.status == 200) {

            var div = document.getElementById("dlg-holder");
            div.innerHTML = xhr.responseText;
            oncomplete();

        } else {
            // handle error
        }
    };

    xhr.send(null);
}
```

So instead of embedding the HTML string in the JavaScript, JavaScript is used to request the string from the server, which allows the markup to be rendered in whatever way is most appropriate before being injected into the page. JavaScript libraries make this process a bit easier by allowing you to load remote markup directly into a DOM element. Both YUI and jQuery have simple APIs for accomplishing this:

```
// YUI
function loadDialog(name, oncomplete) {
    Y.one("#dlg-holder").load("/js/dialog/" + name, oncomplete);
}

// jQuery
function loadDialog(name, oncomplete) {
    $("#dlg-holder").load("/js/dialog/" + name, oncomplete);
}
```

Using remote calls to inject markup is also useful when you need to inject a large amount of HTML into the page. For performance reasons, it's typically not a good idea to keep large amounts of unused markup in memory or in the DOM. For smaller markup chunks, you may want to consider client-side templates.

Alternative #2: Simple Client-Side Templates

Client-side templates are markup pieces with slots that must be filled by JavaScript in order to be complete. For example, a template to add an item to a list might look like this:

```
<li><a href="%s">%s</a></li>
```

This template has `%s` placeholders for the area in which text should be inserted (this is the same format as `sprintf()` from C). The intent is for JavaScript to replace these placeholders with real data before injecting the result into the DOM. Here's the function to use with it:

```
function sprintf(text) {
    var i=1, args=arguments;
    return text.replace(/%s/g, function() {
        return (i < args.length) ? args[i++] : "";
    });
}

// usage
var result = sprintf(templateText, "/item/4", "Fourth item");
```

Getting the template text into JavaScript is an important part of this process. Naturally, you don't want the template text embedded inside of your JavaScript any more than you want markup embedded there. Templates are typically defined in the same area as other markup and are made accessible to JavaScript by embedding them directly in the HTML page, which is done in one of two ways. The first is to include the template as an HTML comment. Comments are DOM nodes just like elements and text, so they can be queried and their content extracted using JavaScript. For example:

```
<ul id="mylist"><!--<li id="item%s"><a href="%s">%s</a></li>-->
    <li><a href="/item/1">First item</a></li>
    <li><a href="/item/2">Second item</a></li>
    <li><a href="/item/3">Third item</a></li>
</ul>
```

The comment is placed in the proper context for its usage, as the first child of the list it will be used in. The following JavaScript retrieves the template text from the comment:

```
var mylist       = document.getElementById("mylist"),
    templateText = mylist.firstChild.nodeValue;
```

Once the template text is retrieved, it just needs to be formatted and inserted into the DOM. All of this is accomplished with the following function:

```
function addItem(url, text) {
    var mylist       = document.getElementById("mylist"),
        templateText = mylist.firstChild.nodeValue,
        result       = sprintf(templateText, url, text);


    mylist.insertAdjacentHTML("beforeend", result);
}

// usage
addItem("/item/4", "Fourth item");
```

This method processes the template text with the given information and then injects the resulting HTML using `insertAdjacentHTML()`. This step turns the HTML string into a DOM node and appends it as a child to the `<ul>`.

The second way of embedding templates into an HTML page is by using a `<script>` element with a custom **type** property. Browsers assume that code in `<script>` elements are JavaScript by default, but you can tell the browser that it is not JavaScript be specifying a **type** that it won't understand. For example:

```
<script type="text/x-my-template" id="list-item">
    <li><a href="%s">%s</a></li>
</script>
```

You can then retrieve the template text by using the **text** property of the `<script>` element:

```
var script       = document.getElementById("list-item"),
    templateText = script.text;
```

The `addItem()` function would then change to:

```
function addItem(url, text) {
    var mylist       = document.getElementById("mylist"),
        script       = document.getElementById("list-item"),
        templateText = script.text,
        result       = sprintf(template, url, text),
        div          = document.createElement("div");
```

```
        div.innerHTML = result.replace(/^\s*/, "");
        mylist.appendChild(div.firstChild);
}

// usage
addItem("/item/4", "Fourth item");
```

One of the changes in this version of the function is to strip any leading white space that may be in the template. This extra white space occurs because the template is on the line after the opening `<script>` tag. Injecting the template as-is would result in a white space text node being created inside `<div>`, and that text node would end up being added to the list instead of the `<li>`.

Alternative #3: Complex Client-Side Templates

The templating format used in the previous section is quite simplistic and doesn't do any escaping. For more robust templating, you may want to consider a solution such as Handlebars (*http://handlebarsjs.com*). Handlebars is a complete client-side templating system designed to work with JavaScript in the browser.

Handlebars templates use double braces to indicate placeholders. Here's a Handlebars version of the template from the previous section:

```
<li><a href="{{url}}">{{text}}</a></li>
```

The placeholders in Handlebars templates are named so that they correspond to named values in JavaScript. Handlebars suggests embedding the template in an HTML page using a `<script>` element with a `type` of text/x-handlebars-template:

```
<script type="text/x-handlebars-template" id="list-item">
    <li><a href="{{url}}">{{text}}</a></li>
</script>
```

To use the template, you first must include the Handlebars JavaScript library on your page, which creates a global variable called `Handlebars` that is used to compile the template text into a function:

```
var script       = document.getElementById("list-item"),
    templateText = script.text,
    template     = Handlebars.compile(script.text);
```

The variable `template` now contains a function that, when executed, returns a formatted string. All you need to do is pass in an object containing the properties `text` and `url`:

```
var result = template({
    text: "Fourth item",
    url: "/item/4"
});
```

As part of formatting the result, the arguments are automatically HTML-escaped, preventing security issues and ensuring that simple text values don't break your markup. For example, the character "&" is automatically escaped to &.

Putting it all together into a single function:

```
function addItem(url, text) {
    var mylist          = document.getElementById("mylist"),
        script          = document.getElementById("list-item"),
        templateText    = script.text,
        template        = Handlebars.compile(script.text),
        div             = document.createElement("div"),
        result;

    result = template({
        text: text,
        url: url
    });

    div.innerHTML = result;
    list.appendChild(div.firstChild);
}

// usage
addItem("/item/4", "Fourth item");
```

This simple example doesn't truly show the flexibility of Handlebars. In addition to simple placeholder replacement, Handlebars allows you to put simple logic and looping into your templates.

Suppose you want to render an entire list rather than an item, but you want to do that only if there are actually items to render. You can create a Handlebars template that looks like this:

```
{{#if items}}
<ul>
    {{#each items}}
    <li><a href="{{url}}">{{text}}</a></li>
    {{/each}}
</ul>
{{/if}}
```

The {{#if}} block helper prevents the enclose markup from being rendered unless the items array has at least one item. The {{#each}} block helper then iterates over each item in the array. So you compile the template into a function and then pass in an object with an items property, as in the following example:

```
// return an empty string
var result = template({
    items: []
});

// return HTML for a list with two items
var result = template({
    items: [
        {
            text: "First item",
            url: "/item/1"
        },
        {
            text: "Second item",
            url: "/item/2"
        }
    ]
});
```

Handlebars has other block helpers as well—all designed to bring powerful templating to JavaScript.

CHAPTER 6

Avoid Globals

The JavaScript execution environment is unique in a lot of ways. One of those ways is in the use of global variables and functions. The default JavaScript execution environment is, in fact, defined by the various globals available to you at the start of script execution. All of these are said to be defined on the *global object*, a mysterious object that represents the outermost context for a script.

In browsers, the `window` object is typically overloaded to also be the global object, so any variable or function declared in the global scope becomes a property of the window object. For example:

```
var color = "red"

function sayColor() {
    alert(color);
}

console.log(window.color);          // "red"
console.log(typeof window.sayColor);  // "function"
```

In this code, the global variable `color` and the global function `sayColor()` are defined. Both are added to the `window` object as properties even though they weren't explicitly set to do so.

The Problems with Globals

Creating globals is considered a bad practice in general and is specifically problematic in a team development environment. Globals create a number of nontrivial maintenance issues for code going forward. The more globals, the greater the possibility that errors will be introduced due to the increasing likelihood of a few common problems.

Naming Collisions

The potential for naming collisions increases as the number of global variables and functions increase in a script, as do the chances that you'll use an already declared variable accidentally. The easiest code to maintain is code in which all of its variables are defined locally.

For instance, consider the sayColor() function from the previous example. This function relies on the global variable color to function correctly. If sayColor() were defined in a separate file than color, it would be hard to track down:

```
function sayColor() {
    alert(color);        // Bad: where'd this come from?
}
```

Further, if color ends up being defined in more than one place, the result of say Color() could be different depending on how this function is included with the other code.

The global environment is where native JavaScript objects are defined, and by adding your own names into that scope, you run the risk of picking a name that might be provided natively by the browser later on. The name color, for example, is definitely not a safe global variable name. It's a plain noun without any qualifiers, so the chances of collision with an upcoming native API, or another developer's work, is quite high.

Code Fragility

A function that depends on globals is tightly coupled to the environment. If the environment changes, the function is likely to break. In the previous example, the say Color() method will throw an error if the global color variable no longer exists. That means any change to the global environment is capable of causing errors throughout the code. Also, globals can be changed at any point by any function, making the reliability of their values highly suspect. The function from the previous example is much more maintainable if color is passed in as an argument:

```
function sayColor(color) {
    alert(color);
}
```

This version of the function has no global dependencies and thus won't be affected by changes to the global environment. Because color is now a named argument, all that matters is that a valid value is passed into the function. Other changes will not affect this function's ability to complete its task.

When defining functions, it's best to have as much data as possible local to the function. Anything that can be defined within the function should be written as such; any data that comes from outside the function should be passed in as an argument. Doing so isolates the function from the surrounding environment and allows you to make changes to either without affecting the other.

Difficulty Testing

I tried to implement some unit testing on one of my first large-scale web applications. I had joined the team after most of the core framework had been built and was trying to get a better understanding of how everything worked in order to create some tests. I was dismayed to discover that creating tests was going to be an extremely difficult process because the entire framework relied on the presence of several global variables to work properly.

Any function that relies on global variables to work requires you to recreate the entire global environment to properly test that function. Effectively, this means that you're not just managing changes in one global environment, you're managing them in two global environments: production and testing. Add to that the cost of keeping those in sync, and you've got the beginnings of a maintenance nightmare that isn't easily untangled.

Ensuring that your functions don't rely on globals improves the testability of your code. Of course, your function may rely on globals that are *native* to JavaScript, such as `Date`, `Array`, and so on. These will always be part of the global environment due to the JavaScript engine. Your functions can always assume that some globals will be present. However, don't allow your functions to become dependent on global variables that you've introduced to ensure optimal testability.

Accidental Globals

One of the more insidious parts of JavaScript is its capacity for creating globals accidentally. When you assign a value to variable that has not previously been defined in a `var` statement, JavaScript automatically creates a global variable. For example:

```
function doSomething() {
    var count = 10;
        title = "Maintainable JavaScript";  // Bad: global

}
```

This code represents a very common coding error that accidentally introduces a global variable. The author probably wanted to declare two variables using a single `var` statement but accidentally included a semicolon after the first variable instead of a comma. The result is the creation of `title` as a global variable.

The problem is compounded when you're trying to create a local variable with the same name as a global variable. For example, a global variable named `count` would be *shadowed* by the local variable `count` in the previous example. The function then has access only to the local `count` unless explicitly accessing the global using `window.count`. This arrangement is actually okay.

Omitting the `var` statement accidentally might mean that you're changing the value of an existing global variable without knowing it. Consider the following:

```
function doSomething() {
    var count = 10;
        name = "Nicholas";  // Bad: global

}
```

In this example, the error is even more egregious because name is actually a property of window by default. When the window.name property is most frequently used with frames or iframes, and is how links are targeted to show up in certain frames or tabs when clicked, changing name inadvertently could affect how links navigate in the site.

A good rule of thumb is to always use var to define variables, even if they are global. This way is a lot less error prone than omitting the var in certain situations.

Avoiding Accidental Globals

JavaScript won't warn when you've accidentally created a global variable by default. That's when tools like JSLint and JSHint come into play. Both tools will warn you if you assign a value to a previously undeclared variable. For example:

```
foo = 10;
```

Both JSLint and JSHint will issue the warning "'foo' is not defined" to let you know that the variable foo was never declared using a var statement.

JSLint and JSHint are also smart enough to notice that you're accidentally changing the value of certain globals. In the example that overwrites the value of name, JSLint and JSHint warn that the variable in question is read-only. In fact, the variable isn't read-only; however, it should be treated as such, because changing a native global almost always leads to errors. The same warning is issued if you try to assign other globals such as window and document.

Strict mode, which changes some of the rules for parsing and executing JavaScript, offers a solution to this problem. By adding "use strict" to the top of a function, you instruct the JavaScript engine to apply more rigorous error handling and syntax checking before executing the code. One of these changes is the ability to detect assignment to undeclared variables. When this happens, the JavaScript engine throws an error. For example:

```
"use strict";
foo = 10;          // ReferenceError: foo is not defined
```

If you try to run this code in an environment supporting strict mode (Internet Explorer 10+, Firefox 4+, Safari 5.1+, Opera 12+, or Chrome), the second will throw a ReferenceError with a message of "foo is not defined."

Turning on strict mode changes a lot of JavaScript behavior, so use it carefully if you're working with older code. For newer code, it's best to always use strict mode to avoid accidental globals as well as other common programming errors that strict mode catches.

The One-Global Approach

You may be thinking at this point, "How is it possible to write JavaScript without introducing any globals?" Although it is technically possible through some clever patterns, this approach is usually not feasible or maintainable in the long run. When JavaScript is developed by a team, that typically means that multiple files are loaded in various scenarios, and the only way to enable communication between this disparate code is to have something that all of the code can rely on to be present. The best approach is to try to have as small a global footprint as possible by agreeing to create only one global object.

The one-global approach is used by all popular JavaScript libraries:

- YUI defines a single YUI global object.
- jQuery actually defines two globals, $ and jQuery. The latter was added only for compatibility when used on a page with other libraries also using $.
- Dojo defines a single dojo global object.
- The Closure library defines a single goog global object.

The idea behind the one-global approach is to create a single global with a unique name (one that is unlikely to be used by native APIs) and then attach all of your functionality onto that one global. So instead of creating multiple globals, each would-be global simply becomes a property of your one global. For instance, suppose I wanted to have an object representing each chapter in this book. The code might look like this:

```
function Book(title) {
    this.title = title;
    this.page = 1;
}

Book.prototype.turnPage = function(direction) {
    this.page += direction;
};

var Chapter1 = new Book("Introduction to Style Guidelines");
var Chapter2 = new Book("Basic Formatting");
var Chapter3 = new Book("Comments");
```

This code creates four globals, Book, Chapter1, Chapter2, and Chapter3. The one-global approach would be to create a single global and attach each of these:

```
var MaintainableJS = {};

MaintainableJS.Book = function(title) {
    this.title = title;
    this.page = 1;
};

MaintainableJS.Book.prototype.turnPage = function(direction) {
    this.page += direction;
};
```

```
MaintainableJS.Chapter1 = new MaintainableJS.Book("Introduction to Style Guidelines");
MaintainableJS.Chapter2 = new MaintainableJS.Book("Basic Formatting");
MaintainableJS.Chapter3 = new MaintainableJS.Book("Comments");
```

This code has a single global, `MaintainableJS`, to which all of the other information is attached. As long as everyone on the team is aware of the single global, it's easy to continue adding properties to it and avoid global pollution.

Namespaces

It is possible to start polluting your one global as well. Most projects that use the one-global approach also have the concept of *namespacing*. A namespace is simply a logical grouping of functionality under a single property on the global. For instance, YUI is set up almost exclusively using namespaces. Everything under `Y.DOM` is a method related to DOM manipulation, everything under `Y.Event` has to do with events, and so on.

Grouping functionality into namespaces brings some order to your one global object and allows team members to understand where new functionality belongs as well as where to look for existing functionality. When I worked at Yahoo!, there was an unspoken convention that each site would add its own namespace to a `Y` object for all of its functionality, so My Yahoo! used `Y.My`, Mail used `Y.Mail`, and so on. That design allowed teams to use one another's code without fear of naming collisions.

You can easily create your own namespaces in JavaScript with objects, as in:

```
var ZakasBooks = {};

// namespace for this book
ZakasBooks.MaintainableJavaScript = {};

// namespace for another book
ZakasBooks.HighPerformanceJavaScript = {}
```

A common convention is for each file to declare its own namespace by creating a new object on the global. In such circumstances, the previous example pattern works fine.

There are also times when each file is simply adding to a namespace; in that case, you may want a little more assurance that the namespace already exists. That's when a global that handles namespaces nondestructively is useful. The basic pattern to accomplish this is:

```
var YourGlobal = {
    namespace: function(ns) {
        var parts = ns.split("."),
            object = this,
            i, len;
```

```
            for (i=0, len=parts.length; i < len; i++) {
                if (typeof object[parts[i]] === "undefined") {
                    object[parts[i]] = {};
                }
                object = object[parts[i]];
            }

            return object;
        }
    };
```

The variable YourGlobal can actually have any name. The important part is the name
space() method, which nondestructively creates namespaces based on the string that
is passed in and returns a reference to the namespace object. Basic usage:

```
/*
 * Creates both YourGlobal.Books and YourGlobal.Books.MaintainableJavaScript.
 * Neither exists before hand, so each is created from scratch.
 */
YourGlobal.namespace("Books.MaintainableJavaScript");

// you can now start using the namespace
YourGlobal.Books.MaintainableJavaScript.author = "Nicholas C. Zakas";

/*
 * Leaves YourGlobal.Books alone and adds HighPerformanceJavaScript to it.
 * This leaves YourGlobal.Books.MaintainableJavaScript intact.
 */
YourGlobal.namespace("Books.HighPerformanceJavaScript");

// still a valid reference
console.log(YourGlobal.Books.MaintainableJavaScript.author);

// You can also start adding new properties right off the method call
YourGlobal.namespace("Books").ANewBook = {};
```

Using a namespace() method on your one global allows developers the freedom to assume that the namespace exists. That way, each file can call namespace() first to declare
the namespace the developers are using, knowing that they won't destroy the namespace if it already exists. This approach also frees developers from the tedious task of
checking to see whether the namespace exists before using it.

As with other parts of your code, be sure to define some conventions
around namespaces. Should they begin with uppercase letters as in YUI?
Or be all lowercase as in Dojo? This is a question of preference, but
defining these choices up front allows the team to use the one-global
approach more effectively.

Modules

Another way developers augment the one-global approach is by using *modules*. A module is a generic piece of functionality that creates no new globals or namespaces. Instead, all of the code takes place within a single function that is responsible for executing a task or publishing an interface. The module may optionally have a name and a list of module dependencies.

Modules aren't formally part of JavaScript. There is no module syntax (at least, not until ECMAScript 6), but there are some common patterns for creating modules. The two most prevalent types are YUI modules and Asynchronous Module Definition (AMD) modules.

YUI modules

YUI modules are, as you might expect, how you create new modules to work with the YUI JavaScript library. The concept of modules was formalized in YUI 3 and takes the following form:

```
YUI.add("module-name", function(Y) {

    // module body

}, "version", { requires: [ "dependency1", "dependency2" ] });
```

YUI modules are added by calling `YUI.add()` with the module name, the function to execute (called a *factory function*), and an optional list of dependencies. The module body is where you place all code for this module. The Y argument is an instance of YUI that has all of the required dependencies available. The YUI convention is to add module functionality as namespaces inside of each module, such as:

```
YUI.add("my-books", function(Y) {

    // Add a namespace
    Y.namespace("Books.MaintainableJavaScript");

    Y.Books.MaintainableJavaScript.author = "Nicholas C. Zakas";

}, "1.0.0", { requires: [ "dependency1", "dependency2" ] });
```

Likewise, the dependencies are represented as namespaces on the Y object that is passed in. So YUI actually combines the concepts of namespaces with modules to give you flexibility in the overall approach.

Use your module via the `YUI().use()` method and pass in one or more module names to load:

```
YUI().use("my-books", "another-module", function(Y) {

    console.log(Y.Books.MaintainableJavaScript.author);

});
```

This code starts by loading the modules named "my-books" and "another-module", ensuring that the dependencies for each are fully loaded. Then the module body is executed in the order in which the modules are specified. Last, the callback function passed to YUI().use() is executed. The Y object that is passed in has all of the changes made to it by the loaded modules, so your application code is ready to execute.

 For more information on YUI modules, see the documentation at *http://yuilibrary.com/yui/docs/yui/*.

Asynchronous Module Definition (AMD) Modules

AMD modules have a lot in common with YUI modules. You specify a module name, dependencies, and a factory function to execute once the dependencies are loaded. These are all passed to a global define() function with the name first, then the dependencies, and then the factory function. A major difference between AMD modules and YUI modules is that each dependency is passed as a separate argument to the factory function. For example:

```
define("module-name", [ "dependency1", "dependency2" ],
        function(dependency1, dependency2) {

    // module body

});
```

So each named dependency ends up creating an object and passing it to the factory function. In this way, AMD seeks to avoid naming collisions that might occur with namespaces across modules. Instead of creating a new namespace as in a YUI module, AMD modules are expected to return their public interface from the factory function, such as:

```
define("my-books", [ "dependency1", "dependency2" ],
        function(dependency1, dependency2) {

    var Books = {};
    Books.MaintainableJavaScript = {
        author: "Nicholas C. Zakas"
    };

    return Books;
});
```

AMD modules can also be anonymous and completely omit the module name. The assumption is that the module loader can infer the module name through the JavaScript filename. So if you have a file named *my-books.js* and your module will only ever be loaded through a module loader, you can define your module as follows:

```
define([ "dependency1", "dependency2" ],
       function(dependency1, dependency2) {

    var Books = {};
    Books.MaintainableJavaScript = {
        author: "Nicholas C. Zakas"
    };

    return Books;
});
```

AMD modules have quite a few options for how to define modules. For more information, see the AMD specification at *https://github.com/amdjs/amdjs-api/wiki/AMD*.

To make use of AMD modules, you need to use a compatible module loader. Dojo's standard module loader supports loading of AMD modules, so you can load a the module "my-books" like this:

```
// load AMD module in Dojo
var books = dojo.require("my-books");

console.log(books.MaintainableJavaScript.author);
```

Dojo also exposes itself as an AMD module named "dojo", so it can be loaded into other AMD modules.

Another module loader is RequireJS (*http://www.requirejs.org*). RequireJS adds another global function called require(), which is responsible for loading the specified dependencies and then executing a callback function. For example:

```
// load AMD module with RequireJS
require([ "my-book" ], function(books) {

    console.log(books.MaintainableJavaScript.author);

});
```

The dependencies start to download immediately upon calling require(), and the callback executes as soon as all of those dependencies have loaded (similar to YUI().use()).

The RequireJS module loader has a lot of logic built in to make loading modules easy. These include mapping of names to directories as well as internationalization options. Both jQuery and Dojo are capable of using RequireJS to load AMD modules.

The Zero-Global Approach

It is possible to inject your JavaScript into a page without creating a single global variable. This approach is quite limited, so it is useful only in some very specific situations. The most common situation is with a completely standalone script that doesn't have to be accessed by any other scripts. This situation may occur because all of the necessary scripts are combined into one file, or because the script is small and being inserted into a page that it shouldn't interfere with. The most common use case is in creating a bookmarklet.

Bookmarklets are unique in that they don't know what's going to be on the page and don't want the page to know that they are present. The end result is a need for a zero-global embedding of the script, which is accomplished by using an immediate function invocation and placing all of the script inside of the function. For example:

```
(function(win) {

    var doc = win.document;

    // declare other variables here

    // other code goes here

}(window));
```

This immediately invoked function passes in the `window` object so that the scripts needn't directly access any global variables. Inside the function, the `doc` variable holds a reference to the `document` object. As long as the function doesn't modify `window` or `doc` directly and all variables are declared using the `var` keyword, this script will result in no globals being injected into the page. You can further avoid creating globals by putting the function into strict mode (for browsers that support it):

```
(function(win) {

    "use strict";

    var doc = win.document;

    // declare other variables here

    // other code goes here

}(window));
```

This function wrapper can now be used for scripts that don't want to create any global objects. As mentioned previously, this pattern is of limited use. Any script that needs to be used by other scripts on the page cannot use the zero-global approach. A script that must be extended or modified during runtime cannot use the zero-global approach, either. However, if you have a small script that doesn't need to interact with any other scripts on the page, the zero-global approach is something to keep in mind.

CHAPTER 7

Event Handling

Event handling is an important part of any JavaScript application. All JavaScript is tied to the UI through events, so most web developers spend much of their time coding and modifying event handlers. Unfortunately, this is also an area of JavaScript programming that hasn't received much attention since the language was first introduced. Even as developers started to embrace more traditional concepts of architecture in JavaScript, event handling was one of those areas in which little has changed. Most event-handling code is very tightly coupled to the event environment (what is available to the developer at the time an event is fired) and therefore is not very maintainable.

Classic Usage

Most developers are familiar with the **event** object that is passed into an event handler when the event is fired. The **event** object contains all of the information related to the event, including the event target as well as additional data based on the event type. Mouse events expose additional location information on the **event** object, keyboard events expose information about keys that have been pressed, and touch events expose information about the location and duration of touches. All of this information is provided so that the UI can react appropriately.

In many cases, however, you end up using a very small subset of the information present on **event**. Consider the following:

```
// Bad
function handleClick(event) {
    var popup = document.getElementById("popup");
    popup.style.left = event.clientX + "px";
    popup.style.top = event.clientY + "px";
    popup.className = "reveal";
}

// addListener() from Chapter 5
addListener(element, "click", handleClick);
```

This code uses just two properties from the event object: `clientX` and `clientY`. These properties are used to position an element on the page before showing it to the user. Even though this code seems relatively simple and unproblematic, it's actually a bad pattern to use in code because of the limitations it imposes.

Rule #1: Separate Application Logic

The previous example's first problem is that the event handler contains *application logic*. Application logic is functionality that is related to the application rather than related to the user's action. In the previous example, the application logic is displaying a pop up in a particular location. Even though this action should happen when the user clicks on a particular element, this may not always be the case.

It's always best to split application logic from any event handler, because the same logic may need to be triggered by different actions in the future. For example, you may decide later that the pop up should be displayed when the user moves the cursor over the element, or when a particular key is pressed on the keyboard. Then you may end up accidentally duplicating the code into a second or third event handler attaching the same event handler to handle multiple events.

Another downside to keeping application logic in the event handler is for testing. Tests need to trigger functionality directly without going through the overhead of actually having someone click an element to get a reaction. By having application logic inside of event handlers, the only way to test is by causing the event to fire. That's usually not the best way to test, even though some testing frameworks are capable of simulating events. It would be better to trigger the functionality with a simple function call.

You should always separate application logic from event-handling code. The first step in refactoring the previous example is to move the pop up–handling code into its own function, which will likely be on the one global object you've defined for your application. The event handler should also be on the same global object, so you end up with two methods:

```
// Better - separate application logic
var MyApplication = {

    handleClick: function(event) {
        this.showPopup(event);
    },

    showPopup: function(event) {
        var popup = document.getElementById("popup");
        popup.style.left = event.clientX + "px";
        popup.style.top = event.clientY + "px";
        popup.className = "reveal";
    }

};
```

```
addListener(element, "click", function(event) {
    MyApplication.handleClick(event);
});
```

The `MyApplication.showPopup()` method now contains all of the application logic previously contained in the event handler. The `MyApplication.handleClick()` method now does nothing but call `MyApplication.showPopup()`. With the application logic separated out, it's easier to trigger the same functionality from multiple points within the application without relying on specific events to fire. But this is just the first step in unraveling this event-handling code.

Rule #2: Don't Pass the Event Object Around

After splitting out application logic, the next problem with the previous example is that the event object is passed around. It's passed from the anonymous event handler to `MyApplication.handleClick()`, then to `MyApplication.showPopup()`. As mentioned previously, the event object has potentially dozens of additional pieces of information about the event, and this code only uses two of them.

Application logic should never rely on the event object to function properly for the following reasons:

- The method interface makes it unclear what pieces of data are actually necessary. Good APIs are transparent in their expectations and dependencies; passing the event object as an argument doesn't give you any idea what it's doing with which pieces of data.

- Because of that, you need to recreate an event object in order to test the method. Therefore, you'll need to know exactly what the method is using to write a proper stub for testing.

These issues are both undesirable in a large-scale web application. Lack of clarity is what leads to bugs.

The best approach is to let the event handler use the event object to handle the event and then hand off any required data to the application logic. For example, the `MyApplication.showPopup()` method requires only two pieces of data: an x-coordinate and a y-coordinate. The method should then be rewritten to accept those as arguments:

```
// Good
var MyApplication = {

    handleClick: function(event) {
        this.showPopup(event.clientX, event.clientY);
    },

    showPopup: function(x, y) {
        var popup = document.getElementById("popup");
        popup.style.left = x + "px";
        popup.style.top = y + "px";
```

```
            popup.className = "reveal";
        }

    };

    addListener(element, "click", function(event) {
        MyApplication.handleClick(event);    // this is okay
    });
```

In this rewritten code, MyApplication.handleClick() now passes in the x-coordinate
and y-coordinate to MyApplication.showPopup() instead of passing the entire event object. It's very clear what MyApplication.showPopup() expects to be passed in, and it's
quite easy to call that logic directly from a test or elsewhere in the code, such as:

```
    // Great victory!
    MyApplication.showPopup(10, 10);
```

When handling events, it is best to let the event handler be the only function that
touches the event object. The event handler should do everything necessary using the
event object before delegating to some application logic. Thus actions such as preventing the default action or stopping event bubbling should be done strictly in the
event handler, as in:

```
    // Good
    var MyApplication = {

        handleClick: function(event) {

            // assume DOM Level 2 events support
            event.preventDefault();
            event.stopPropagation();

            // pass to application logic
            this.showPopup(event.clientX, event.clientY);
        },

        showPopup: function(x, y) {
            var popup = document.getElementById("popup");
            popup.style.left = x + "px";
            popup.style.top = y + "px";
            popup.className = "reveal";
        }

    };

    addListener(element, "click", function(event) {
        MyApplication.handleClick(event);    // this is okay
    });
```

In this code, MyApplication.handleClick() is the defined event handler, so it makes the
calls to event.preventDefault() and event.stopPropagation() before passing data to
the application logic, which is exactly how the relationship between event handlers and
the application should work. Because the application logic no longer depends on
event, it's easy to use that same logic in multiple places as well as to write tests.

CHAPTER 8

Avoid Null Comparisons

A common yet still problematic pattern in JavaScript is testing a variable against `null`, presumably to determine whether the variable has been filled in with an appropriate value. For example:

```
var Controller = {
    process: function(items) {
        if (items !== null) {      // Bad
            items.sort();
            items.forEach(function(item) {
                // do something
            });
        }
    }
};
```

Here, the `process()` method is clearly expecting that `items` will be an array, as indicated by the use of `sort()` and `forEach()`. The intention of this code is clear: don't continue processing unless the `items` argument contains an array. The problem with this approach is that the comparison against `null` doesn't actually prevent future errors. The value of `items` could be 1, or a string, or some random object. All of these are technically not equal to `null` and would therefore cause the `process()` method to fail once `sort()` executes.

Comparing a variable against only `null` typically doesn't give you enough information about the value to determine whether it's safe to proceed. Fortunately, JavaScript gives you a number of ways to determine the true value of a variable.

Detecting Primitive Values

There are five primitive types in JavaScript: string, number, boolean, `null`, and `undefined`. If you are expecting a value to be a string, number, boolean, or `undefined`, then the `typeof` operator is your best option. The `typeof` operator works on a variable and returns a string indicating the type of value:

- For strings, typeof returns "string".
- For numbers, typeof returns "number".
- For booleans, typeof returns "boolean".
- For undefined, typeof returns "undefined".

Basic syntax for typeof is as follows:

```
typeof variable
```

You may also see typeof used in this manner:

```
typeof(variable)
```

Although this is valid JavaScript syntax, this pattern makes typeof appear to be a function instead of an operator. For this reason, the pattern without parentheses is recommended.

Using typeof for detecting these four primitive value types is the safest way to code defensively. Here are some examples:

```
// detect a string
if (typeof name === "string") {
    anotherName = name.substring(3);
}

// detect a number
if (typeof count === "number") {
    updateCount(count);
}

// detect a boolean
if (typeof found === "boolean" && found) {
    message("Found!");
}

// detect undefined
if (typeof MyApp === "undefined") {
    MyApp = {
        // code
    };
}
```

The typeof operator is also unique in that it can be used on an undeclared variable without throwing an error. Both undeclared variables and variables whose value is undefined return "undefined" when typeof is used.

The last primitive type, null, is the one that you normally shouldn't be testing for. As stated earlier, comparing simply against null generally doesn't give you enough information about whether the value is expected. There is one exception: if one of the expected values is actually null, then it is okay to test for null directly. The comparison should be done using either === or !== against null. For example:

```
// If you must test for null, this is the way to do it
var element = document.getElementById("my-div");
if (element !== null) {
    element.className = "found";
}
```

It is entirely possible for document.getElementById() to return null if the given DOM element isn't found. The method will return either null or an element. Because null is one of the expected outcomes, it's okay to test for it using !==.

 Running typeof null returns "object", making this an inefficient way to test for null values. If you must test for null, use the identically equal operator (===) or the not identically equal (!==) operator.

Detecting Reference Values

Reference values are also known as *objects*. In JavaScript, any value that isn't a primitive is definitely a reference. There are several built-in reference types such as Object, Array, Date, and Error, just to name a few. The typeof operator is of little use for reference values, because it returns "object" for any type of object:

```
console.log(typeof {});            // "object"
console.log(typeof []);            // "object"
console.log(typeof new Date());    // "object"
console.log(typeof new RegExp());  // "object"
```

Another downside to using typeof for objects is that typeof returns "object" for null values as well:

```
console.log(typeof null);          // "object"
```

This quirk, which has been recognized as a serious bug in the specification, prevents accurate detection of null using typeof.

The instanceof operator is the best way to detect values of a particular reference type. Basic syntax for instanceof is:

```
value instanceof constructor
```

Here are some examples:

```
// detect a Date
if (value instanceof Date) {
    console.log(value.getFullYear());
}

// detect a RegExp
if (value instanceof RegExp) {
    if (value.test(anotherValue)) {
        console.log("Matches");
    }
}
```

```
// detect an Error
if (value instanceof Error) {
    throw value;
}
```

An interesting feature of `instanceof` is that it not only checks the constructor used to create the object but also checks the prototype chain. The prototype chain contains information about the inheritance pattern used to define the object. For instance, every object inherits from `Object` by default, so every object returns true for `value instanceof Object`. For example:

```
var now = new Date();

console.log(now instanceof Object);    // true
console.log(now instanceof Date);      // true
```

Due to this behavior, it's typically not good enough to use `value instanceof Object` when you're expecting a particular type of object.

The `instanceof` operator also works with custom types that you've defined for yourself. For instance:

```
function Person(name) {
    this.name = name;
}

var me = new Person("Nicholas");

console.log(me instanceof Object);    // true
console.log(me instanceof Person);    // true
```

This example creates a custom `Person` type. The `me` variable is an instance of `Person`, so `me instanceof Person` is true. As mentioned previously, all objects are also considered instances of `Object`, so `me instanceof Object` is also true.

The `instanceof` operator is the only good way to detect custom types in JavaScript. It's also good to use for almost all built-in JavaScript types. There is, however, one serious limitation.

Suppose that an object from one browser frame (frame A) is passed into another (frame B). Both frames have the constructor function `Person` defined. If the object from frame A is an instance of `Person` in frame A, then the following rules apply:

```
// true
frameAPersonInstance instanceof frameAPerson

// false
frameAPersonInstance instanceof frameBPerson
```

Because each frame has its own copy of `Person`, it is considered an instance of only that frame's copy of `Person`, even though the two definitions may be identical.

This issue is a problem not just for custom types but also for two very important built-in types: functions and arrays. For these two types, you don't want to use `instanceof` at all.

Detecting Functions

Functions are technically reference types in JavaScript and also technically have a `Function` constructor of which each function is an instance. For example:

```
function myFunc() {}

// Bad
console.log(myFunc instanceof Function);        // true
```

However, this approach doesn't work across frames due to each frame having its own `Function` constructor. Fortunately, the `typeof` operator also works with functions, returning "function":

```
function myFunc() {}

// Good
console.log(typeof myFunc === "function");      // true
```

Using `typeof` is the best way to detect functions, because it also works across frames.

There is one limitation to `typeof`'s function detection. In Internet Explorer 8 and earlier, any functions that are part of the DOM (such as `document.getElementById()`) return "object" instead of "function" when used with `typeof`. For instance:

```
// Internet Explorer 8 and earlier
console.log(typeof document.getElementById);        // "object"
console.log(typeof document.createElement);         // "object"
console.log(typeof document.getElementsByTagName);  // "object"
```

This quirk arises due to how the browser implements the DOM. In short, these early versions of Internet Explorer didn't implement the DOM as native JavaScript functions, which caused the native `typeof` operator to identify the functions as objects. Because the DOM is so well defined, developers typically test for DOM functionality using the `in` operator, understanding that the presence of the object member means that it's a function, as in:

```
// detect DOM method
if ("querySelectorAll" in document) {
    images = document.querySelectorAll("img");
}
```

This code checks to see whether `querySelectorAll` is defined in `document`, and if so, goes on to use that function. Though not ideal, this is the safest way to check for the presence of DOM methods if you need to support Internet Explorer 8 and earlier. In all other cases, the `typeof` operator is the best way to detect functions in JavaScript.

Detecting Arrays

Passing arrays back and forth between frames was one of the original cross-frame issues in JavaScript. Developers quickly discovered that `instanceof Array` didn't always produce appropriate results in these cases. As mentioned previously, each frame has its own `Array` constructor, so an instance from one frame isn't recognized in another. Douglas Crockford first recommended performing some *duck typing*, testing for the presence of the `sort()` method:

```
// Duck typing arrays
function isArray(value) {
    return typeof value.sort === "function";
}
```

This detection relies on the fact that arrays are the only object types with a `sort()` method. Of course, this version of `isArray()` will also return true when any object with a `sort()` method is passed in.

There was quite a lot of investigation into accurately detecting array types in JavaScript; ultimately, Juriy Zaytsev (also known as Kangax) proposed an elegant solution to this problem:

```
function isArray(value) {
    return Object.prototype.toString.call(value) === "[object Array]";
}
```

Kangax found that calling the native `toString()` method on a given value produced a standard string in all browsers. For arrays, the string is "[object Array]", and this call worked regardless of the frame from which the array originated. Kangax's approach quickly became popular and is now implemented in most JavaScript libraries.

 This approach is generally useful for identifying native objects as opposed to developer-defined objects. For example, the native `JSON` object returns "[object JSON]" using this technique.

Since that time, ECMAScript 5 has introduced `Array.isArray()` formally into JavaScript. The sole purpose of this method is to accurately determine whether a value is an array. As with Kangax's function, `Array.isArray()` works with values that are passed across frames, so many JavaScript libraries now implement methods similar to this:

```
function isArray(value) {
    if (typeof Array.isArray === "function") {
        return Array.isArray(value);
    } else {
        return Object.prototype.toString.call(value) === "[object Array]";
    }
}
```

The `Array.isArray()` method is implemented in Internet Explorer 9+, Firefox 4+, Safari 5+, Opera 10.5+, and Chrome.

Detecting Properties

Another time when when developers typically use `null` (and also `undefined`) is when trying to determine whether a property is present in an object. For example:

```
// Bad: Checking falsyness
if (object[propertyName]) {
    // do something
}

// Bad: Compare against null
if (object[propertyName] != null) {
    // do something
}

// Bad: Compare against undefined
if (object[propertyName] != undefined) {
    // do something
}
```

Each of these examples is actually checking the value of the property with the given name rather than the existence of the property with the given name, which can result in errors when you're dealing with falsy values such as 0, "" (empty string), `false`, `null`, and `undefined`. After all, these are all valid values for properties. For example, if the property is keeping track of a number, the value might very well be zero. In that case, the first example will likely cause a bug. Likewise, if the property value could be `null` or `undefined`, all three examples can cause bugs.

The best way to detect the presence of a property is to use the `in` operator. The `in` operator simply checks for the presence of the named property without reading its value, avoiding ambiguity with statements such as those earlier in this section. If the property either exists on the instance or is inherited from the object's prototype, the `in` operator returns `true`. For example:

```
var object = {
    count: 0,
    related: null
};

// Good
if ("count" in object) {
    // this executes
}

// Bad: Checking falsy values
if (object["count"]) {
    // this doesn't execute
}

// Good
if ("related" in object) {
    // this executes
}
```

```
// Bad: Checking against null
if (object["related"] != null) {
    // doesn't execute
}
```

If you only want to check for the existence of the property on the object instance, then use the hasOwnProperty() method. All JavaScript objects that inherit from Object have this method, which returns true when the property exists on the instance (if the property only exists on the prototype, in which case it returns false). Keep in mind that DOM objects in Internet Explorer 8 and earlier do not inherit from Object and therefore do not have this property. That means you'll need to check for the existence of hasOwn Property() before using it on potential DOM objects (if you know the object isn't from the DOM, you can omit this step).

```
// Good for all non-DOM objects
if (object.hasOwnProperty("related")) {
    //this executes
}

// Good when you're not sure
if ("hasOwnProperty" in object && object.hasOwnProperty("related")) {
    //this executes
}
```

Because of Internet Explorer 8 and earlier, I tend to use the in operator whenever possible and only use hasOwnProperty() when I need to be sure of an instance property.

Whenever you want to check for the existence of the property, make sure to use the in operator or hasOwnProperty(). Doing so can avoid a lot of bugs.

 Of course, if you want to specifically check for the values of null or undefined, use the guidelines in Chapter 1.

CHAPTER 9

Separate Configuration Data from Code

Code does nothing more than define a set of instructions for a computer to execute. Data is frequently passed around and modified by those instructions, ultimately producing a result. The problem comes when the data must change. There's a risk of creating an error any time you edit source code, and editing code just to change some data value introduces unnecessary risk for something that shouldn't affect the surrounding instructions. Well-designed applications keep vital data outside of the main source code to ensure worry-free editing.

What Is Configuration Data?

Configuration data is any hardcoded value in an application. Consider the following example:

```
// Configuration data embedded in code
function validate(value) {
    if (!value) {
        alert("Invalid value");
        location.href = "/errors/invalid.php";
    }
}

function toggleSelected(element) {
    if (hasClass(element, "selected")) {
        removeClass(element, "selected");
    } else {
        addClass(element, "selected");
    }
}
```

There are three pieces of configuration data in this code. The first is the string "Invalid value," which is displayed to the user. As a UI string, there's a good chance that it will change frequently. The second is the URL */errors/invalid.php*. URLs tend to change as development progresses, due to architectural decisions. The third is the CSS class name "selected." This class name is used three times, meaning that a class name change requires changes in three different places, increasing the likelihood that one will be missed.

These are all considered configuration data, because they are hardcoded values that may change in the future. The following are all examples of configuration data:

- URLs
- Strings that are displayed in the UI
- Repeated unique values
- Settings (i.e., items per page)
- Any value that may change

The key point to remember about configuration data is that it changes, and you don't want to be modifying your JavaScript source code because someone changed his mind about a message to display on the home page.

Externalizing Configuration Data

The first step in separating configuration data from code is to externalize the configuration data, which means getting the data out of the middle of your JavaScript code. Here's the previous example with the configuration data externalized:

```
// Configuration data externalized
var config = {
    MSG_INVALID_VALUE:  "Invalid value",
    URL_INVALID:        "/errors/invalid.php",
    CSS_SELECTED:       "selected"
};

function validate(value) {
    if (!value) {
        alert(config.MSG_INVALID_VALUE);
        location.href = config.URL_INVALID;
    }
}

function toggleSelected(element) {
    if (hasClass(element, config.CSS_SELECTED)) {
        removeClass(element, config.CSS_SELECTED);
    } else {
        addClass(element, config.CSS_SELECTED);
    }
}
```

This example stores all of the configuration data in the config object. Each property of config holds a single piece of data, and each property name has a prefix indicating the type of data (MSG for a UI message, URL for a URL, and CSS for a class name). The naming convention is, of course, a matter of preference. The important part of this code is that all of the configuration data has been removed from the functions and replaced with placeholders from the config object.

Externalizing the configuration data means that anyone can go in and make a change without introducing an error in the application logic. It also means that the entire config object can be moved into its own file, so edits are made far away from the code that uses the data.

Storing Configuration Data

Configuration data is best stored in a separate file to create a clean separation between it and application logic. A good starting point is to have a separate JavaScript file for configuration data. Once the configuration data is in a separate file, it opens up more possibilities for managing that data. A worthwhile option is moving your configuration data into a non-JavaScript file.

Even though you're writing a JavaScript application, JavaScript isn't a great way to store configuration data. That's because the syntax is still that of a programming language, so you need to be sure you haven't introduced syntax errors. If you end up concatenating JavaScript files together, a syntax error in a single line breaks the overall application. Configuration data truly belong in files that are hard to format incorrectly, and once you have that file, it is trivial to convert the configuration data into a JavaScript format automatically.

One of my favorite formats for configuration data is a Java properties file. Java properties files are simple name-value pairs in which each pair takes a single line (unless you put in a multiple-line sequence) in the form name=value. It doesn't matter if there are spaces around the equals sign, so even that syntax isn't hard to get right. Comments are indicated by preceding the line with a # character. Here's an example:

```
# UI Strings
MSG_INVALID_VALUE = Invalid value

# URLs
URL_INVALID = /errors/invalid.php

# CSS Classes
CSS_SELECTED = selected
```

This properties file contains the same properties as the config object from the previous example. Notice how much simpler the file layout is. There are no quoted strings, which means that you don't have to worry about proper escaping or forgetting to close a string. There are also no semicolons or commas to worry about. You can simply put in your data and not worry about JavaScript syntax at all.

The next step is to convert this file into something that's usable by JavaScript. There are generally three formats in which you want your configuration data. The first is

JSON, which is useful when embedding your data into another file or setting up data for retrieval from the server. For instance:

```
{"MSG_INVALID_VALUE":"Invalid value","URL_INVALID":"/errors/invalid.php",
"CSS_SELECTED":"selected"}
```

The second is JSONP (JSON with padding), which returns the JSON structure wrapped in a function:

```
myfunc({"MSG_INVALID_VALUE":"Invalid value","URL_INVALID":"/errors/invalid.php",
        "CSS_SELECTED":"selected"});
```

Because JSONP is valid JavaScript, you can concatenate this code into other files to give them access to the data.

The last option is plain JavaScript, in which you assign the JSON object to a variable to use later, as in:

```
var config={"MSG_INVALID_VALUE":"Invalid value","URL_INVALID":"/errors/invalid.php",
            "CSS_SELECTED":"selected"};
```

As with JSONP, the plain JavaScript version can be combined with other JavaScript files easily once produced.

For these common use cases, I have created a tool called Props2Js that reads Java properties files and outputs the data into one of these three formats. Props2Js is free and open source, available at *https://github.com/nzakas/props2js/*. It works like this:

```
java -jar props2js-0.1.0.jar --to jsonp --name myfunc
    --output result.js source.properties
```

The `--to` option specifies the output format, either "js," "json," or "jsonp." The `--name` option specifies either the variable name (for "js") or the function name (for "jsonp"); this option is ignored for "json." The `--output` option specifies the file to write the data into. So this line takes the Java properties file named *source.properties* and outputs JSONP with a callback function of `myfunc` to a file named *result.js*.

Using a tool like Props2Js allows you to keep configuration data in a simpler file format and then easily convert your configuration data into a format that is usable by JavaScript later.

CHAPTER 10

Throw Your Own Errors

When I was younger, the most befuddling part of programming languages was the ability to create errors. My first reaction to the `throw` operator in Java was, "Well, that's stupid; why would you ever want to *cause* an error?" Errors were my enemy—something I sought to avoid—so the ability to cause an error seemed like a useless and dangerous aspect of the language. I thought it was dumb to include the same operator in JavaScript, a language that people just didn't understand in the first place. Now, with a great deal of experience under my belt, I'm a big fan of throwing my own errors.

Throwing errors in JavaScript is an art. It takes time to feel out where the appropriate parts of your code should throw errors. Once you figure this out, however, you'll find that your debugging time will decrease and your satisfaction with the code will increase.

The Nature of Errors

An error occurs in programming when something unexpected happens. Maybe the incorrect value was passed into a function or a mathematical operation had an invalid operand. Programming languages define a base set of rules that when deviated from, result in errors so that the developer can fix the code. Debugging would be nearly impossible if errors weren't thrown and reported back to you. If everything failed silently, it would take you a long time to notice that there was an issue in the first place, let alone isolate and fix it. Errors are the friends of developers, not enemies.

The problem with errors is that they tend to pop up in unexpected places and at unexpected times. To make matters worse, the default error messages are usually too terse to really explain what went wrong. JavaScript error messages are notoriously uninformative and cryptic (especially in old versions of Internet Explorer), which only compounds the problem. Imagine if an error popped up with a message that said, "This function failed because this happened." Instantly, your debugging task becomes easier. This ease is the advantage of throwing your own errors.

It helps to think of errors as built-in failure cases. It's always easier to plan for a failure at a particular point in code than it is to anticipate failure everywhere. This is a very common practice in product design, not just in code. Cars are built with crumple zones, areas of the frame that are designed to collapse in a predictable way when impacted. Knowing how the frame will react in a crash—specifically, which parts will fail—allows the manufacturers to ensure passenger safety. Your code can be constructed in the same way.

Throwing Errors in JavaScript

Throwing errors in your JavaScript is arguably more valuable than in any other language due to the complexities involved in web debugging. You can throw an error by using the `throw` operator and providing an object to throw. Any type of object can be thrown; however, an `Error` object is the most typical to use:

```
throw new Error("Something bad happened.")
```

The built-in `Error` type is available in all JavaScript implementations, and the constructor takes a single argument, which is the error message. When you throw an error in this way, and the error isn't caught via a `try-catch` statement, the browser displays the value of `message` in the browser's typical way. Most browsers now have a console to which error information is output whenever an error occurs. In other words, any error you throw is treated the same way as an error that you didn't throw.

Inexperienced developers sometimes throw errors by just providing a string, such as:

```
// Bad
throw "message";
```

Doing so will cause an error to be thrown, but not all browsers respond the way you'd expect. Firefox, Opera, and Chrome each display an "uncaught exception" message and then include the message string. Safari and Internet Explorer simply throw an "uncaught exception" error and don't provide the message string at all, which isn't very useful for debugging purposes.

Of course, you can throw any type of data that you'd like. There are no rules prohibiting specific data types:

```
throw { name: "Nicholas" };
throw true;
throw 12345;
throw new Date();
```

The only thing to remember is that throwing any value will result in an error if it's not caught via a `try-catch` statement. Firefox, Opera, and Chrome all call `String()` on the value that was thrown to display something logical as the error message; Safari and Internet Explorer do not. The only surefire way to have all browsers display your custom error message is to use an `Error` object.

Advantages of Throwing Errors

Throwing your own error allows you to provide the exact text to be displayed by the browser. Instead of just line and column numbers, you can include any information that you'll need to successfully debug the issue. I recommend that you always include the function name in the error message as well as the reason why the function failed. Consider the following function:

```
function getDivs(element) {
    return element.getElementsByTagName("div");
}
```

This function's purpose is to retrieve all `<div>` elements that are a descendant of `element`. It's quite common for functions that interact with the DOM to be passed `null` values where DOM elements should be. What happens if `null` is passed to this function? You'll get a cryptic error message such as "object expected." Then you'll need to look at the execution stack to actually locate the source of the problem. Debugging becomes much easier by throwing an error:

```
function getDivs(element) {

    if (element && element.getElementsByTagName) {
        return element.getElementsByTagName("div");
    } else {
        throw new Error("getDivs(): Argument must be a DOM element.");
    }
}
```

Now that `getDivs()` throws an error, any time `element` doesn't meet the criteria for continuing, an error is thrown that very clearly states the problem. If this error shows up in the browser console, you know immediately where to start debugging and that the most likely cause is a call to retrieve a DOM element is returning `null` at some point.

I like to think of throwing errors as leaving sticky notes for myself as to why something failed.

When to Throw Errors

Understanding how to throw errors is just one part of the equation; understanding when to throw errors is the other. Because JavaScript doesn't have type or argument checking, a lot of developers incorrectly assume that they should implement these types of checking for every function. Doing so is impractical and can adversely affect the script's overall performance. Consider this function, which tries to implement overly aggressive type checking:

```
// Bad: Too much error checking
function addClass(element, className) {
    if (!element || typeof element.className != "string") {
        throw new Error("addClass(): First argument must be a DOM element.");
    }

    if (typeof className != "string") {
        throw new Error("addClass(): Second argument must be a string.");
    }

    element.className += " " + className;
}
```

This function simply adds a CSS class to a given element; however, most of the function is taken up doing error checking. Even though it may be tempting to check each argument in every function (mimicking statically typed languages), doing so is often overkill in JavaScript. The key is to identify parts of the code that are likely to fail in a particular way and throw errors only there. In short, throw errors only where errors will already occur.

The most likely cause of an error in the previous example is a null reference being passed in to the function. If the second argument is null, or a number, or a boolean, no error will be thrown, because JavaScript will coerce the value into a string. That may mean that the resulting display of the DOM element isn't as expected, but it certainly doesn't rise to the level of serious error. So I would check only for the DOM element, as in:

```
// Good
function addClass(element, className) {
    if (!element || typeof element.className != "string") {
        throw new Error("addClass(): First argument must be a DOM element.");
    }

    element.className += " " + className;
}
```

If a function is only ever going to be called by known entities, error checking is probably unnecessary (this is the case with private functions); if you cannot identify all the places where a function will be called ahead of time, then you'll likely need some error checking and will even more likely benefit from throwing your own errors. The best place for throwing errors is in utility functions, such as the addClass() function, that are a general part of the scripting environment and may be used in any number of places, which is precisely the case with JavaScript libraries.

All JavaScript libraries should throw errors from their public interfaces for known error conditions. Large libraries such as jQuery, YUI, and Dojo can't possibly anticipate when and where you'll be calling their functions. It's their job to tell you when you're doing stupid things, because you shouldn't have to debug into library code to figure out what went wrong. The call stack for an error should terminate in the library's interface and no deeper. There's nothing worse than seeing an error that's 12 functions deep into a library; library developers have a responsibility to prevent this from happening.

The same goes for private JavaScript libraries. Many web applications have their own proprietary JavaScript libraries either built with or in lieu of the well-known public options. The goal of libraries is to make developers' lives easier, which is done by providing an abstraction away from the dirty implementation details. Throwing errors helps to keep those dirty implementation details hidden safely away from developers.

Some good general rules of thumb for throwing errors:

- Once you've fixed a hard-to-debug error, try to add one or two custom errors that can help you more easily solve the problem, should it occur again.
- If you're writing code and think, "I hope [something] doesn't happen—that would really mess up this code," then throw an error when that something occurs.
- If you're writing code that will be used by people you don't know, think about how they might incorrectly use the function and throw errors in those cases.

Remember that the goal isn't to prevent errors—it's to make errors easier to debug when they occur.

The try-catch Statement

JavaScript provides a try-catch statement that is capable of intercepting thrown errors before they are handled by the browser. The code that might cause an error comes in the try block and code that handles the error goes into the catch block. For instance:

```
try {
    somethingThatMightCauseAnError();
} catch (ex) {
    handleError(ex);
}
```

When an error occurs in the try block, execution immediately stops and jumps to the catch block, where the error object is provided. You can inspect this object to determine the best course of action to recover from the error.

There is also a finally clause that can be added. The finally clause contains code that will be executed regardless of whether an error occurs. For example:

```
try {
    somethingThatMightCauseAnError();
} catch (ex) {
    handleError(ex);
} finally {
    continueDoingOtherStuff();
}
```

The finally clause is a little bit tricky to work with in certain situations. For example, if the try clause contains a return statement, it won't actually return until finally has been evaluated. Due to this trickiness, `finally` is used infrequently, but it is a powerful tool for error handling if necessary.

Throw or try-catch?

Typically, developers have trouble discerning whether it's appropriate to throw an error or catch one using `try-catch`. Errors should be thrown only in the deepest part of the application stack, which, as discussed previously, typically means JavaScript libraries. Any code that handles application-specific logic should have error-handling capabilities and should therefore be catching errors thrown from the lower-level components.

Application logic always knows why it was calling a particular function and is therefore best suited for handling the error. Never have a `try-catch` statement with an empty `catch` clause; you should always be handling errors in some way. For example, never do this:

```
// Bad
try {
    somethingThatMightCauseAnError();
} catch (ex) {
    // noop
}
```

If you know an error might happen, then you should also know how to recover from that error. Exactly how you recover from the error may be different in development mode as opposed to what actually gets put into production, and that's okay. The important thing is that you're actually handling the error, not just ignoring it.

Error Types

ECMA-262 specifies seven error object types. These are used by the JavaScript engine when various error conditions occur and can also be manually created:

Error
: Base type for all errors. Never actually thrown by the engine.

EvalError
: Thrown when an error occurs during execution of code via `eval()`.

RangeError
: Thrown when a number is outside the bounds of its range—for example, trying to create an array with –20 items (`new Array(-20)`). These errors rarely occur during normal execution.

ReferenceError
: Thrown when an object is expected but not available—for instance, trying to call a method on a `null` reference.

SyntaxError
: Thrown when the code passed into `eval()` has a syntax error.

TypeError
>   Thrown when a variable is of an unexpected type—for example, `new 10` or `"prop"` in `true`.

URIError
>   Thrown when an incorrectly formatted URI string is passed into `encodeURI`, `encodeURIComponent`, `decodeURI`, or `decodeURIComponent`.

Understanding that there are different types of errors can make it easier to handle them. All error types inherit from `Error`, so checking the type with `instanceof Error` doesn't give you any useful information. By checking for the more specific error types, you get more robust error handling:

```
try {
    // something that causes an error
} catch (ex) {
    if (ex instanceof TypeError) {
        // handle the error
    } else if (ex instanceof ReferenceError) {
        // handle the error
    } else {
        // handle all others
    }
}
```

If you're throwing your own errors, and you're throwing a data type that isn't an error, you can more easily tell the difference between your own errors and the ones that the browser throws. There are, however, several advantages to throwing actual `Error` objects instead of other object types.

First, as mentioned before, the error message will be displayed in the browser's normal error-handling mechanism. Second, the browser attatches extra information to `Error` objects when they are thrown. These vary from browser to browser, but they provide contextual information for the error such as line number and column number and, in some browsers, stack and source information. Of course, you lose the ability to distinguish between your own errors and browser-thrown ones if you just use the `Error` constructor.

The solution is to create your own error type that inherits from `Error`. Doing so allows you to provide additional information as well as distinguish your errors from the errors that the browser throws. You can create a custom error type using the following pattern:

```
function MyError(message) {
    this.message = message;
}

MyError.prototype = new Error();
```

There are two important parts of this code: the `message` property, which is necessary for browsers to know the actual error string, and setting the prototype to an instance of `Error`, which identifies the object as an error to the JavaScript engine. Now you can throw an instance of `MyError` and have the browser respond as if it's a native error:

```
throw new MyError("Hello world!");
```

The only caveat to this approach is that Internet Explorer 8 and earlier won't display the error message. Instead, you'll see the generic "Exception thrown but not caught" error message. The big advantage of this approach is that custom error objects allow you to test specifically for your own errors:

```
try {
    // something that causes an error
} catch (ex) {
    if (ex instanceof MyError) {
        // handle my own errors
    } else {
        // handle all others
    }
}
```

If you're always catching any errors you throw, then Internet Explorer's slight stupidity shouldn't matter all that much. The benefits from such an approach are huge in a system with proper error handling. This approach gives you much more flexibility and information for determining the correct course of action for a given error.

CHAPTER 11

Don't Modify Objects You Don't Own

One unique aspect of JavaScript is that nothing is sacred. By default, you can modify any object you can get your hands on. It doesn't matter if the object is developer-defined or part of the default execution environment—it's possible to change that object as long as you have access to it. This isn't a problem in a one-developer project, in which exactly what is being modified is always known by the one person who's in control of all code. On a multiple-developer project, however, the indiscriminate modification of objects is a big problem.

What Do You Own?

You own an object when your code creates the object. The code that creates the object may not have necessarily been written by you, but as long as it's the code you're responsible for maintaining, then you own that object. For instance, the YUI team owns the `YUI` object, and the Dojo team owns the `dojo` object. Even though the original person who wrote the code defining the object may not work on it anymore, the respective teams are still the owners of those objects.

When you use a JavaScript library in a project, you don't automatically become the owner of its objects. In a multiple-developer project, everyone is assuming that the library objects work as they are documented. If you're using YUI and make modifications to the `YUI` object, then you're setting up a trap for your team. Someone is going to fall in, and it's going to cause a problem.

Remember, if your code didn't create the object, then it's not yours to modify, which includes:

- Native objects (`Object`, `Array`, and so on)
- DOM objects (for example, `document`)
- Browser Object Model (BOM) objects (such as `window`)
- Library objects

All of these objects are part of your project's execution environment. You can use these pieces as they are already provided to you or create new functionality; you should not modify what's already there.

The Rules

Enterprise software needs a consistent and dependable execution environment to be maintainable. In other languages, you consider existing objects as libraries for you to use to complete your task. In JavaScript, you might see existing objects as a playground in which you can do anything you want. You should treat the existing JavaScript objects as you would a library of utilities:

- Don't override methods.
- Don't add new methods.
- Don't remove existing methods.

When you're the only one working on a project, it's easy to get away with these types of modification because you know them and expect them. When working with a team on a large project, making changes like this causes mass confusion and a lot of lost time.

Don't Override Methods

One of the worst practices in JavaScript is overriding a method on an object you don't own, which is precisely what caused us problems when I worked on the My Yahoo! team. Unfortunately, JavaScript makes it incredibly easy to override an existing method. Even the most venerable of methods, `document.getElementById()`, can be easily overridden:

```
// Bad
document.getElementById = function() {
    return null;        // talk about confusing
};
```

There is absolutely nothing preventing you from overwriting DOM methods as in this example. What's worse, any script on the page is capable of overwriting any other script's methods. So any script could override `document.getElementById()` to always return `null`, which in turn would cause JavaScript libraries and other code that relies upon this method to fail. You've also completely lost the original functionality and can't get it back.

You may also see a pattern like this:

```
// Bad
document._originalGetElementById = document.getElementById;
document.getElementById = function(id) {
    if (id == "window") {
        return window;
    } else {
```

```
        return document._originalGetElementById(id);
    }
};
```

In this example, a pointer to the original `document.getElementById()` is stored in `docu ment._originalGetElementById()` so that it can be used later. Then, `document.getEle mentById()` is overridden to contain a new method. That new method may call the original in some cases, but in one case, it won't. This override-plus-fallback pattern is at least as bad as the original, and perhaps worse because sometimes `docu ment.getElementById()` behaves as expected and sometimes it doesn't.

I have firsthand experience dealing with the fallout after someone overrides an existing object method. It occurred while I was working on the My Yahoo! team, because someone had overridden the YUI 2 `YAHOO.util.Event.stopEvent()` method to do something else. It took days to track this problem down, because we all assumed that this method was doing exactly what it always did, so we never traced into that method once we hit it in a debugger. Once we discovered the overridden method, we also found other bugs, because the same method was being used in other places with its original intended usage—but of course it wasn't behaving in that way. Unraveling this was an incredible mess, one that cost a lot of time and money on a big project.

Don't Add New Methods

It's quite easy to add new methods to existing objects in JavaScript. You need only assign a function onto an existing object to make it a method, which allows you to modify all kinds of objects:

```
// Bad - adding method to DOM object
document.sayImAwesome = function() {
    alert("You're awesome.");
};

// Bad - adding method to native object
Array.prototype.reverseSort = function() {
    return this.sort().reverse();
};

// Bad - adding method to library object
YUI.doSomething = function() {
    // code
};
```

There is little stopping you from adding methods to any object you come across. The big problem with adding methods to objects you don't own is that you may end up with a naming collision. Just because an object doesn't have a method right now doesn't mean it won't in the future. What's worse is that if the future native method behaves differently than your method, then you have a maintenance nightmare.

Take a lesson from the history of the Prototype JavaScript library. Prototype was famous for modifying all kinds of JavaScript objects. It added methods to DOM and native objects at will; in fact, most of the library was defined as extensions to existing objects rather than by creating their own. The Prototype developers saw the library as a way of filling in JavaScript's gaps. Prior to version 1.6, Prototype implemented a method called `document.getElementsByClassName()`. You may recognize this method, because it was officially defined in HTML5 to standardize Prototype's approach.

Prototype's `document.getElementsByClassName()` method returned an array of elements containing the specified CSS classes. Prototype also had added a method on arrays, `Array.prototype.each()`, which iterated over the array and executed a function on each item. This led to developers writing code such as:

```
document.getElementByClassName("selected").each(doSomething);
```

This code didn't have a problem until HTML5 standardized the method and browsers began implementing it natively. The Prototype team knew the native `document.getEle mentsByClassName()` was coming, so they did some defensive coding similar to the following:

```
if (!document.getElementsByClassName) {

    document.getElementsByClassName = function(classes) {
        // non-native implementation
    };

}
```

So Prototype was defining `document.getElementsByClassName()` only if it didn't already exist. That would have been the end of the issue except for one important fact. The HTML5 `document.getElementsByClassName()` didn't return an array, so the `each()` method didn't exist. Native DOM methods use a specialized collection type called `NodeList`, and `document.getElementsByClassname()` returned a `NodeList` to match the other DOM methods.

Because `NodeList` doesn't have an `each()` method, either natively or added by Prototype, using `each()` caused a JavaScript error when executed in browsers that had a native implementation of `document.getElementsByClassName()`. The end result was that users of Prototype had to upgrade both the library code and their own code—quite the maintenance nightmare.

Learn from Prototype's mistake. You cannot accurately predict how JavaScript will change in the future. As the standards have evolved, they have often taken cues from JavaScript libraries such as Prototype to determine the next generation of functionality. In fact, a native `Array.prototype.forEach()` method is defined in ECMAScript 5 that works much like Prototype's `each()` method. The problem is that you don't know how the official functionality will differ from the original, and even subtle differences can cause big problems.

Most JavaScript libraries have a plugin architecture that allows you to safely add new capabilities to the libraries. If you want to modify a library, creating a plug-in is the best and most maintainable way to do so.

Don't Remove Methods

It's just as easy to remove JavaScript methods as it is to add then. Of course, overriding a method is one form of removing an existing method. The simplest way to eliminate a method is to set its name equal to `null`:

```
// Bad - eliminating a DOM method
document.getElementById = null;
```

Setting a method to `null` ensures that it can't be called, regardless of how it was defined. If the method is defined on the object instance (as opposed to the object prototype), then it can also be removed using the `delete` operator:

```
var person = {
    name: "Nicholas"
};

delete person.name;

console.log(person.name);      // undefined
```

This example removes the `name` property from the `person` object. The `delete` operator works only on instance properties and methods. If `delete` is used on a prototype property or method, it has no effect. For example:

```
// No effect
delete document.getElementById;

console.log(document.getElementById("myelement"));  // stil works
```

Because `document.getElementById()` is a prototype method, it cannot be removed using `delete`. However, as seen in an earlier example, it can still be set to `null` to prevent access.

It should go without saying that removing an already existing method is a bad practice. Not only are developers relying on that method to be there, but code may already exist using that method. Removing a method that is in use causes a runtime error. If your team shouldn't be using a particular method, mark it as deprecated, either through documentation or through static code analysis. Removing a method should be the absolute last approach.

Not removing methods is actually a good practice for objects that you own, as well. It's very hard to remove methods from libraries or native objects, because there is third-party code relying on that functionality. In many cases, both libraries and browsers have had to keep buggy or incomplete methods for a long time, because removing them would cause errors on countless websites.

Better Approaches

Modifying objects you don't own is a solution to some problems. It usually doesn't happen organically; it happens because a developer has come across a problem that object modification solves. However, there is almost always more than one solution to any given problem. Most computer science knowledge has evolved out of solving problems in statically typed languages such as Java. There are many approaches, called *design patterns*, to extending existing objects without directly modifying those objects.

The most popular form of object augmentation outside of JavaScript is inheritance. If there's a type of object that does most of what you want, then you can inherit from it and add additional functionality. There are two basic forms of inheritance in JavaScript: object-based and type-based.

 There are still some significant inheritance limitations in JavaScript. First, inheriting from DOM or BOM objects doesn't work (yet). Second, inheriting from `Array` doesn't quite work due to the intricacies of how numeric indices relate to the `length` property.

Object-Based Inheritance

In object-based inheritance, frequently called *prototypal inheritance*, one object inherits from another without invoking a constructor function. The ECMAScript 5 `Object.create()` method is the easiest way for one object to inherit from another. For instance:

```
var person = {
    name: "Nicholas",
    sayName: function() {
        alert(this.name);
    }
};

var myPerson = Object.create(person);

myPerson.sayName();     // pops up "Nicholas"
```

This example creates a new object `myPerson` that inherits from `person`. The inheritance occurs as `myPerson`'s prototype is set to `person`. After that, `myPerson` is able to access the same properties and methods on `person` until new properties or methods with the same name are defined. For instance, defining `myPerson.sayName()` automatically cuts off access to `person.sayName()`:

```
myPerson.sayName = function() {
    alert("Anonymous");
};

myPerson.sayName();     // pops up "Anonymous"
person.sayName();       // pops up "Nicholas"
```

The `Object.create()` method allows you to specify a second argument, which is an object containing additional properties and methods to add to the new object. For example:

```
var myPerson = Object.create(person, {
    name: {
        value: "Greg"
    }
});

myPerson.sayName();     // pops up "Greg"
person.sayName();       // pops up "Nicholas"
```

In this example, `myPerson` is created with its own value for `name`, so calling `sayName()` displays "Greg" instead of "Nicholas."

Once a new object is created in this manner, you are completely free to modify the new object in whatever manner you see fit. After all, you are the owner of the new object, so you are free to add new methods, override existing methods, and even remove methods (or rather just prevent access to them) on your new object.

Type-Based Inheritance

Type-based inheritance works in a similar manner to object-based inheritance, in that it relies on the prototype to inherit from an existing object. However, type-based inheritance works with constructor functions instead of objects, which means you need access to the constructor function of the object you want to inherit from. You saw an example of type-based inheritance earlier in this book:

```
function MyError(message) {
    this.message = message;
}

MyError.prototype = new Error();
```

In this example, the `MyError` type inherits from `Error`, which is called the *super type*. It does so by assigning a new instance of `Error` to `MyError.prototype`. After that, every instance of `MyError` inherits its properties and methods from `Error` as well as now working with `instanceof`:

```
var error = new MyError("Something bad happened.");

console.log(error instanceof Error);        // true
console.log(error instanceof MyError);       // true
```

Type-based inheritance is best used with developer-defined constructor functions rather than those found natively in JavaScript. Also, type-based inheritance typically requires two steps: prototypal inheritance and then constructor inheritance. Constructor inheritance is when the super type constructor is called with a `this`-value of the newly created object. For example:

```
function Person(name) {
    this.name;
}

function Author(name) {
    Person.call(this, name);     // inherit constructor
}

Author.prototype = new Person();
```

In this code, the `Author` type inherits from `Person`. The property `name` is actually managed by the `Person` type, so `Person.call(this, name)` allows the `Person` constructor to continue defining that property. The `Person` constructor runs on `this`, which is the new `Author` object. So `name` ends up being defined on the new `Author` object.

As with object-based inheritance, type-based inheritance allows you flexibility in how you create new objects. Defining a type allows you to have multiple instances of the same object, all of which inherit from a common super type. Your new type should define exactly the properties and methods you want to use, and those can be completely different from the super type.

The Facade Pattern

The facade pattern is a popular design pattern that creates a new interface for an existing object. A facade is a completely new object that works with an existing object behind the scenes. Facades are also sometimes called **wrappers**, because they wrap an existing object with a different interface. If inheritance won't work for your use case, then creating a facade is the next logical step.

Both jQuery and YUI use facades for their DOM interfaces. As mentioned previously, you can't inherit from DOM objects, so the only option for safely adding new functionality is to create an facade. Here's an example DOM object wrapper:

```
function DOMWrapper(element) {
    this.element = element;
}

DOMWrapper.prototype.addClass = function(className) {
    this.element.className += " " + className;
};
```

```
DOMWrapper.prototype.remove = function() {
    this.element.parentNode.removeChild(this.element);
};

// Usage
var wrapper = new DOMWrapper(document.getElementById("my-div"));

// add a CSS class
wrapper.addClass("selected");

// remove the element
wrapper.remove();
```

The DOMWrapper type expects a DOM element to be passed into its constructor. That element is stored so that it can be referenced later, and methods are defined that work on that element. The addClass() method is an easy way to add CSS classes for elements not yet implementing the HTML5 classList property. The remove() method encapsulates removing an element from the DOM, eliminating the need for the developer to access the element's parent node.

Facades are well suited to maintainable JavaScript, because you have complete control over the interface. You can allow or disallow access to any of the underlying object's properties or methods, effectively filtering access to that object. You can also add new methods that are simpler to use than the existing ones (as is the case in this example). If the underlying object changes in any way, you're able to make changes to the facade that allow your application to continue working.

 A facade that implements a specific interface to make one object look like it's another is called an *adapter*. The only difference between facades and adapters is that the former creates a new interface and the latter implements an existing interface.

A Note on Polyfills

JavaScript *polyfills* (also known as *shims*) became popular when ECMAScript 5 and HTML5 features started being implemented in browsers. A polyfill implements functionality that is already well-defined and implemented natively in newer browsers. For example, ECMAScript 5 added the forEach() method for arrays. This method can be implemented using ECMAScript 3, so older browsers can use forEach() as if it were a newer browser. The key to polyfills is that they implement native functionality in a completely compatible way. Because the functionality exists in some browsers, it's possible to test whether different cases are handled in a standards-compliant manner.

Polyfills often add new methods to objects they don't own to achieve their end goal. I'm not a fan of polyfills, but I do understand why people use them. Polyfills are marginally safer than other types of object modification, because the native implementation already exists and can be worked with. Polyfills add new methods only when the native one isn't present and the nonnative version behaves the same as the native one.

The advantage of polyfills is that you can easily remove them when you're supporting only browsers with the native functionality. If you choose to use a polyfill, do your due diligence. Make sure the functionality matches the native version as closely as possible and double-check that the library has unit tests to verify the functionality. The disadvantage of polyfills is that they may not accurately implement the missing functionality, and then you end up with more problems rather than fewer.

For best maintainability, avoid polyfills and instead create a facade over existing native functionality. This approach gives you the most flexibility, which is especially important when native implementations have bugs. In that case, you never want to use the native API directly, because you can't insulate yourself from the implementation bugs.

Preventing Modification

ECMAScript 5 introduced several methods to prevent modification of objects. This capability is important to understand, as it's now possible to lock down objects to ensure that no one, accidentally or otherwise, changes functionality that they shouldn't. This functionality is supported in Internet Explorer 9+, Firefox 4+, Safari 5.1+, Opera 12+, and Chrome. There are three levels of preventing modification:

Prevent extension
> No new properties or methods can be added to the object, but existing ones can be modified or deleted.

Seal
> Same as prevent extension, plus prevents existing properties and methods from being deleted.

Freeze
> Same as seal, plus prevents existing properties methods from being modified (all fields are read-only).

Each of these lock-down types has two methods: a method that performs the action and a method that confirms the action was taken. For preventing extensions, `Object.preventExtensions()` and `Object.isExtensible()` are used:

```
var person = {
    name: "Nicholas"
};

// lock down the object
Object.preventExtensions(person);

console.log(Object.isExtensible(person));      // false
```

```
person.age = 25;     // fails silently unless in strict mode
```

In this example, person is locked down to the extension, so Object.isExtensible() is false. Attempting to assign a new property or method will fail silently in nonstrict mode. In strict mode, any attempt to add a new property or method to a nonextensible object causes an error.

To seal an object, use Object.seal(). You can determine whether an object is sealed using Object.isSealed():

```
// lock down the object
Object.seal(person);

console.log(Object.isExtensible(person));    // false
console.log(Object.isSealed(person));        // true

delete person.name; // fails silently unless in strict mode
person.age = 25;     // fails silently unless in strict mode
```

When an object is sealed, its existing properties and methods cannot be removed, so attempting to remove name will fail silently in nonstrict mode. In strict mode, attempting to delete a property or method results in an error. Sealed objects are also nonextensible, so Object.isExtensible() returns false.

To freeze an object, use Object.freeze(). You can determine whether an object is frozen using Object.isFrozen():

```
// lock down the object
Object.freeze(person);

console.log(Object.isExtensible(person));    // false
console.log(Object.isSealed(person));        // true
console.log(Object.isFrozen(person));        // true

person.name = "Greg";    // fails silently unless in strict mode
person.age = 25;         // fails silently unless in strict mode
delete person.name;      // fails silently unless in strict mode
```

Frozen objects are considered both nonextensible and sealed, so Object.isExtensible() returns false and Object.isSealed() returns true for all frozen objects. The big difference between frozen objects and sealed objects is that you cannot modify any existing properties or methods. Any attempt to do so fails silently in nonstrict mode and throws an error in strict mode.

Preventing modification using these ECMAScript 5 methods is an excellent way to ensure that your objects aren't modified without your knowledge. If you're a library author, you may want to lock down certain parts of the core library to make sure they're not accidentally changed or to enforce where extensions are allowed to live. If you're an application developer, lock down any parts of the application that shouldn't change. In both cases, using one of the lock-down methods should happen only *after* you've completely defined all object functionality. Once an object is locked down, it cannot be restored.

If you decide to prevent modification of your objects, I strongly recommend using strict mode. In nonstrict mode, attempts to modify unmodifiable objects always fail silently, which could be very frustrating during debugging. By using strict mode, these same attempts will throw an error and make it more obvious why the modification isn't working.

 It's likely that in the future, both native JavaScript and DOM objects will have some built-in protection against modification using this ECMAScript 5 functionality.

CHAPTER 12

Browser Detection

Browser detection is always a hot-button topic in web development. This battle predates JavaScript browser detection by a couple of years and begins with the introduction of Netscape Navigator, the first truly popular and widely used web browser. Netscape Navigator 2.0 was so far beyond any of the other available web browsers that websites began looking for its specific user-agent string before returning any useful content. This forced other browser vendors, notably Microsoft, to include things in their user-agent string to get around this form of browser detection.

User-Agent Detection

The earliest form of browser detection was *user-agent detection*, a process by which the server (and later the client) looked at the user-agent string and determined the browser. During that time, servers would regularly block certain browsers from viewing anything on the site based solely on the user-agent string. The browser that benefited the most was Netscape Navigator. Netscape was certainly the most capable browser, so websites targeted that browser as the only one that could properly display the site. Netscape's user-agent string looked like this:

```
Mozilla/2.0 (Win95; I)
```

When Internet Explorer was first released, it was essentially forced to duplicate a large part of the Netscape user-agent string to ensure that servers would serve up the site to this new browser. Because most user-agent detection was done by searching for "Mozilla" and then taking the version number after the slash, the Internet Explorer user-agent string was:

```
Mozilla/2.0 (compatible; MSIE 3.0; Windows 95)
```

Internet Explorer's introduction meant that everyone's user-agent string detection method identified Internet Explorer as Netscape. This started a trend of new browsers partially copying the user-agent strings of existing browsers that continued up through the release of Chrome, whose user-agent string contains parts of Safari's string, which in turn contained parts of Firefox's string, which in turn contained parts of Netscape's string.

Fast forward to the year 2005, when JavaScript started to increase in popularity. The browser's user-agent string, the same one reported to the server, is accessible in JavaScript through `navigator.userAgent`. User-agent string detection moved into web pages with JavaScript performing the same type of user-agent string detection as the server, such as:

```
// Bad
if (navigator.userAgent.indexOf("MSIE") > -1) {
    // it's Internet Explorer
} else {
    // it's not
}
```

As more websites took to user-agent detection in JavaScript, a new group of sites started to fail in browsers. The same problem for bit servers nearly a decade earlier had reemerged in the form of JavaScript.

The big problem is that user-agent string parsing is difficult, due to the way browsers have copied one another to try to ensure compatibility. With every new browser, user-agent detection code needs to be updated, and the time between the browser is released to the time the changed code is deployed could mean untold numbers of people getting a bad user experience.

This isn't to say that there isn't any way to use the user-agent string effectively. There are well-written libraries, both in JavaScript and for the server, that provide a reasonably good detection mechanism. Unfortunately, these libraries also require constant updates as browsers continue to evolve and new browsers are released. The overall approach isn't maintainable over the long term.

User-agent detection should always be the last approach to determining the correct course of action in JavaScript. If you choose user-agent detection, then the safest way to proceed is by detecting only older browsers. For instance, if you need to do something special to make your code work in Internet Explorer 8 and earlier, then you should detect Internet Explorer 8 and earlier rather than trying to detect Internet Explorer 9 and higher, such as:

```
if (isInternetExplorer8OrEarlier) {
    // handle IE8 and earlier
} else {
    // handle all other browsers
}
```

The advantage you have in this situation is that the Internet Explorer 8 and earlier user-agent strings are well known and won't be changing. Even if your code continues to run through the release of Internet Explorer 25, the code will most likely continue to work without further modifications. The opposite isn't true—you'll be stuck updating code constantly if you try to detect Internet Explorer 9 and higher.

Browsers don't always report their original user-agent string. User-agent switchers are readily available for nearly all web browsers. Developers are frequently concerned about this and therefore won't turn to user-agent detection, even when it's the only option, because "you can never know for sure." My advice is not to worry about user-agent spoofing. If a user is savvy enough to switch her user-agent string, then she's also savvy enough to understand that doing so might cause websites to break in unforeseen ways. If the browser identifies itself as Firefox and doesn't act like Firefox, that's not your fault. There's no point in trying to second-guess the reported user-agent string.

Feature Detection

Looking to use a more sane approach to browser-based conditionals, developers turned to a technique called *feature detection*. Feature detection works by testing for a specific browser feature and using it only if present. So instead of doing something like this:

```
// Bad
if (navigator.userAgent.indexOf("MSIE 7") > -1) {
    // do something
}
```

you should do something like this:

```
// Good
if (document.getElementById) {
    // do something
}
```

There is a distinction between these two approaches. The first is testing for a specific browser by name and version; the second is testing for a specific feature, namely docu ment.getElementById. So user-agent sniffing results in knowing the exact browser and version being used (or at least the one being reported by the browser) and feature detection determines whether a given object or method is available. Note that these are two completely different results.

Because feature detection doesn't rely on knowledge of which browser is being used, only on which features are available, it is trivial to ensure support in new browsers. For instance, when the DOM was young, not all browsers supported document.getElement ById(), so there was a lot of code that looked like this:

```
// Good
function getById (id) {

    var element = null;

    if (document.getElementById) {     // DOM
        element = document.getElementById(id);
    } else if (document.all) {         // IE
        element = document.all[id];
    } else if (document.layers) {      // Netscape <= 4
        element = document.layers[id];
    }

    return element;
}
```

This is a good and appropriate use of feature detection, because the code tests for a feature and then, if it's there, uses it. The test for document.getElementById() comes first because it is the standards-based solution. After that come the two browser-specific solutions. If none of these features is available, then the method simply returns null. The best part about this function is that when Internet Explorer 5 and Netscape 6 were released with support for document.getElementById(), this code didn't need to change.

The previous example illustrates several important parts of good feature detection:

1. Test for the standard solution
2. Test for browser-specific solutions
3. Provide a logical fallback if no solution is available

The same approach is used today with the cutting-edge features that browsers have implemented experimentally while the specification is being finalized. For instance, the requestAnimationFrame() method was being finalized toward the end of 2011, at which time several browsers had already implemented their own version with a vendor prefix. The proper feature detection for requestAnimationFrame() looks like this:

```
// Good
function setAnimation (callback) {

    if (window.requestAnimationFrame) {                  // standard
        return requestAnimationFrame(callback);
    } else if (window.mozRequestAnimationFrame) {        // Firefox
        return mozRequestAnimationFrame(callback);
    } else if (window.webkitRequestAnimationFrame) {     // WebKit
        return webkitRequestAnimationFrame(callback);
    } else if (window.oRequestAnimationFrame) {          // Opera
        return oRequestAnimationFrame(callback);
    } else if (window.msRequestAnimationFrame) {         // IE
        return msRequestAnimationFrame(callback);
    } else {
        return setTimeout(callback, 0);
    }

}
```

This code starts by looking for the standard `requestAnimationFrame()` method, and only if it's not found does it continue to look for the browser-specific implementation. The very last option, for browsers with no support, is to use `setTimeout()` instead. Once again, this code won't need to be updated even after the browsers have switched to using a standards-based implementation.

Avoid Feature Inference

One inappropriate use of feature detection is called *feature inference*. Feature inference attempts to use multiple features after validating the presence of only one. The presence of one feature is inferred by the presence of another. The problem is, of course, that inference is an assumption rather than a fact, and that can lead to maintenance issues. For example, here's some older code using feature inference:

```
// Bad - uses feature inference
function getById (id) {

    var element = null;

    if (document.getElementsByTagName) {    // DOM
        element = document.getElementById(id);
    } else if (window.ActiveXObject) {    // IE
        element = document.all[id];
    } else {                              // Netscape <= 4
        element = document.layers[id];
    }

    return element;
}
```

This function is feature inference at its worst. There are several inferences being made:

*   If `document.getElementsByTagName()` is present, then `document.getElementById()` is present. In essence, this assumption is inferring from the presence of one DOM method that all DOM methods are available.
*   If `window.ActiveXObject` is present, then `document.all` is present. This inference basically says that `window.ActiveXObject` is present only for Internet Explorer, and `document.all` is also present only in Internet Explorer, so if you know one is there then the other must also be there. In fact, some versions of Opera supported `document.all`.
*   If neither of these inferences is true, then it must be Netscape Navigator 4 or earlier. This isn't strictly true.

You cannot infer the existence of one feature based on the existence of another feature. The relationship between two features is tenuous at best and circumstantial at worst. It's like saying, "If it looks like a duck, then it must quack like a duck."

Avoid Browser Inference

Somewhere along the lines, a lot of web developers grew confused about the distinction between user-agent detection and feature detection. Code started being written similar to this:

```
// Bad
if (document.all) {  // IE
    id = document.uniqueID;
} else {
    id = Math.random();
}
```

The problem with this code is that a test for `document.all` is used as an implicit check for Internet Explorer. Once it's known that the browser is Internet Explorer, the assumption is that it's safe to use `document.uniqueID`, which is IE-specific. However, all you tested was whether `document.all` is present, not whether the browser is Internet Explorer. Just because `document.all` is present doesn't mean that `document.uniqueID` is also available. There's a false implication that can cause the code to break.

As a clearer statement of this problem, developers started replacing code like this:

```
var isIE = navigator.userAgent.indexOf("MSIE") > -1;
```

With code like this:

```
// Bad
var isIE = !!document.all;
```

Making this change indicates a misunderstanding of "don't use user-agent detection." Instead of looking for a particular browser, you're looking for a feature and then trying to infer that it's a specific browser, which is just as bad. This is called *browser inference* and is a very bad practice.

Somewhere along the line, developers realized that `document.all` was not, in fact, the best way to determine whether a browser was Internet Explorer. The previous code was replaced with more specific code, such as this:

```
// Bad
var isIE = !!document.all && document.uniqueID;
```

This approach falls into the "too clever" category of programming. You're trying too hard to identify something by describing an increasing number of identifying aspects. What's worse is that there's nothing preventing other browsers from implementing the same capabilities, which will ultimately make this code return unreliable results.

Browser inference even made it into some JavaScript libraries. The following snippet comes from MooTools 1.1.2:

```
// from MooTools 1.1.2
if (window.ActiveXObject)
    window.ie = window[window.XMLHttpRequest ? 'ie7' : 'ie6'] = true;
else if (document.childNodes && !document.all && !navigator.taintEnabled)
```

```
        window.webkit = window[window.xpath ? 'webkit420' : 'webkit419'] = true;
    else if (document.getBoxObjectFor != null || window.mozInnerScreenX != null)
        window.gecko = true;
```

This code tries to determine which browser is being used based on browser inference. There are several problems with this code:

- Internet Explorer 8, which supports both `window.ActiveXObject` and `window.XMLHttpRequest`, will be identified as Internet Explorer 7.

- Any browser that implements `document.childNodes` is likely to be reported as Web-Kit if it's not already identified as Internet Explorer.

- The number of WebKit versions being identified is far too small, and once again, WebKit 422 and higher will be incorrectly reported as WebKit 422.

- There is no check for Opera, so either Opera will be incorrectly reported as one of the other browsers, or it won't be detected at all.

- This code will need to be updated whenever a new browser is released.

The number of issues with the browser inference code is quite daunting, especially the last one. For every new browser release, MooTools would have had to update this code and get it pushed out to all users quite quickly to avoid code breaking. That's just not maintainable in the long run.

To understand why browser inference doesn't work, you need only look back to high school math class, in which logic statements are typically taught. Logic statements are made up of a hypothesis (p) and a conclusion (q) in the form "if p, then q." You can try altering the statement form to determine truths. There are three ways to alter the statement:

- Converse: if q, then p
- Inverse: if not p, then not q
- Contrapositive: if not q, then not p

There are two important relationships among the various forms of the statement. If the original statement is true, then the contrapositive is also true. For example, if the original statement was "If it's a car, then it has wheels" (which is true) then the contrapositive, "if it doesn't have wheels, then it's not a car," is also true.

The second relationship is between the converse and the inverse, so if one is true, then the other must also be true. This makes sense logically, because the relationship between converse and inverse is the same as between original and contrapositive.

Perhaps more important than these two relationships are the relationships that don't exist. If the original statement is true, then there is no guarantee that the converse is true. This is where feature-based browser detection falls apart. Consider this true statement: "If it's Internet Explorer, then `document.all` is implemented." The contrapositive, "If `document.all` is not implemented, then it's not Internet Explorer," is also true. The converse, "If `document.all` is implemented, then it's Internet Explorer," is not strictly true (some versions of Opera implemented it). Feature-based detection assumes that the converse is always true when, in fact, there is no such relationship.

Adding more parts to the conclusion doesn't help, either. Consider once again the statement, "If it's a car, then it has wheels." The converse is obviously false: "If it has wheels, then it's a car." You could try making it more precise: "If it's a car, then it has wheels and requires fuel." Check the converse: "If it has wheels and requires fuel, then it's a car." Also not true, because an airplane fits that description. So try again: "If it's a car, then it has wheels, requires fuel, and uses two axles." Once again, the converse isn't going to be true.

The problem is fundamental to human language: it's very hard to use a collection of singular aspects to define the whole. We have the word "car" because it implies a lot of aspects that you would otherwise have to list to identify that thing in which you drive to work. Trying to identify a browser by naming more and more features is the exact same problem. You'll get close, but it will never be a reliable categorization.

MooTools backed themselves, and their users, into a corner by opting for feature-based browser detection. Mozilla had warned since Firefox 3 that the `getBoxObjectFor()` method was deprecated and would be removed in a future release. Because MooTools relied on this method to determine whether a browser is Gecko-based, Mozilla's removal of the method in Firefox 3.6 meant that anyone running older versions of MooTools could have code that was now affected. This situation prompted MooTools to issue a call to upgrade to the most recent version, in which the issue is "fixed." The explanation:

> We have overhauled our browser detection to be based on the user agent string. This has become the standard practice among JavaScript libraries because of potential issues, as Firefox 3.6 demonstrates. As browsers grow closer together, looking at features to separate them will become more difficult and risky. From this point forward, browser detection will only be used where it would be impossible not to, in order to give the consistent experience across browsers that one would expect from a world-class JavaScript framework.

What Should You Use?

Feature inference and browser inference are very bad practices that should be avoided at all costs. Straight feature detection is a best practice, and in almost every case, is exactly what you'll need. Typically, you just need to know if a feature is implemented before using it. Don't try to infer relationships between features, because you'll end up with false positives or false negatives.

I won't go so far as to say never use user-agent detection, because I do believe there are valid use cases. I don't believe, however, that there are a lot of valid use cases. If you're thinking about user-agent sniffing, keep this in mind: the only safe way to do so is to target older versions of a specific browser. You should never target the most current browser version or future versions.

My recommendation is to use feature detection whenever possible. If it's not possible, then fall back to user-agent detection. Never, ever use browser inference, because you'll be stuck with code that isn't maintainable and will constantly require updating as browsers continue to evolve.

PART III

Automation

> "I . . . am rarely happier than when spending an entire day programming my computer to perform automatically a task that would otherwise take me a good ten seconds to do by hand." —Douglas Adams, *Last Chance to See*

Prior to the year 2000, it was quite common for web developers to simply put their JavaScript files onto a web server in the same form as they had in source control, comments and all. If there were 10 files in source control, then there were also 10 files on the server. This type of mirroring, in which what you had locally and what you had on the server were identical, allowed for rapid changes. Additionally, this led to the "view source" era, where many web developers learned from going to a site and then viewing the source of the page along with its JavaScript.

Of course, during that time the amount of JavaScript found on websites was still quite small compared to today's standards. Whereas a hundred lines of JavaScript code written by a single developer used to be the norm, today's modern web applications often have thousands of lines of JavaScript being modified by a dozen or more developers. Needless to say, the old way of doing things just doesn't work any longer.

All large-scale (and many small-scale) web applications rely on automation for processing their JavaScript files. Automation is quite common with other parts of a web application stack, but until 2005, hadn't been popularly used for JavaScript. Adding JavaScript into the overall web application automation system is an important step for maintainability, allowing you to have the same type of safeguards as other parts of the system.

Advantages and Disadvantages

The advantages of using an automated build system for your JavaScript are:

- The code you have in source control doesn't have to mirror what is put out into production, so you can set up source control any way you want without having to worry about whether it's optimized for use on the server.

- Static analysis can be performed automatically to find errors.
- JavaScript can be processed in any number of ways before deployment, including concatenation of files and minification.
- Testing is automated, so problems can easily be identified.
- Automatic deployment into production servers is easy.
- You can easily and quickly rerun common tasks.

Using such automation does come with some disadvantages as well:

- Developers might need to run a local build while making changes in a development environment. Some developers have a lot of trouble adjusting to this step, having grown used to making changes and just refreshing the browser.
- The code that is deployed to production doesn't look like the code that is being edited, making bugs in production harder to track down.
- Developers who are less technical may have trouble using the build system.

In my experience, the advantages of having automation in place far outweigh the disadvantages. Even those developers who hate the idea of needing to run a local build after making changes tend to come around once the advantages of the system have been realized.

CHAPTER 13

File and Directory Structure

The first step before setting up a build system is to determine how your files and directories are laid out. This structure is heavily affected by the type of project. If the project is a standalone JavaScript library, you might want a different structure than you would want for a project containing all of the files for a website.

Best Practices

Regardless of the project type, there are several best practices that apply to JavaScript file and directory structure:

One object per file
> Each JavaScript file should contain code for just one JavaScript object. This pattern is common to other programming languages and generally makes maintenance easier. Having multiple files with single objects reduces the risk of multiple people working on the same file at the same time. Even though today's source control systems are incredibly good at merging changes from two different people, merge conflicts do still occur. The fewer files you have, the greater the likelihood of merge conflicts. Keeping one JavaScript object per file minimizes this risk.

Group related files in directories
> If you have multiple objects that are related, put all of those files into a single directory. You might, for instance, have multiple files with code to make a single module. It makes sense to have a directory just for that module containing all of the files. Grouping related files helps developers locate functionality easily.

Keep third-party code separate
> Any code that isn't being written or maintained by you, such as a JavaScript library, should be kept in a separate part of source control. In fact, the ideal setup is not to have the JavaScript library checked in at all but rather to load it directly from a Content Delivery Network (CDN). In lieu of that, keeping the files in a separate directory within source control is the best approach.

Determine build location

> The location of the built JavaScript files should be a completely separate directory that is not checked in to source control. The website should be configured to use this build location instead of the source directory. It's important to not check in built files because these are artifacts of the build system, artifacts that may be re-created multiple times by multiple people or systems before finally being deployed. The deployment should kick off a build that creates the final artifacts to be deployed.

Keep test code close

> Your JavaScript testing code should also be checked in to source control and be in a predictable location. This makes it easy for developers to notice when tests are missing.

File and directory structure are a bit different if the JavaScript you're working on is part of a larger website or web application versus a standalone JavaScript project. The overall directory structure is typically dictated by the server-side framework being used. Even though the overall directory structure may vary from project to project, you will undoubtedly have a subdirectory devoted just to JavaScript. This subdirectory may be called *scripts* or *javascript*, but there is almost always a single directory devoted to JavaScript files. Within that directory, there are a few common layouts.

Basic Layout

One popular layout style is to have three primary directories in your JavaScript directory:

build

> For the final built files. Ideally, shouldn't be checked in.

src

> For all of the source files. Contains subdirectories for grouping files.

test or tests

> For all of the test files. Usually contains some subdirectory structure or file structure that mirrors that of *src*.

CSS Lint (*https://github.com/stubbornella/csslint*), a project that I manage, uses a variation of this approach. See Figure 13-1.

For CSS Lint, the *build* directory is never checked in; however, the *release* directory always contains the most recent stable release. The *src* directory has several subdirectories, grouping related functionality together. The *tests* directory mirrors the directory structure of *src*, so the tests for *src/core/CSSLint.js* are found in *tests/core/CSSLint.js*.

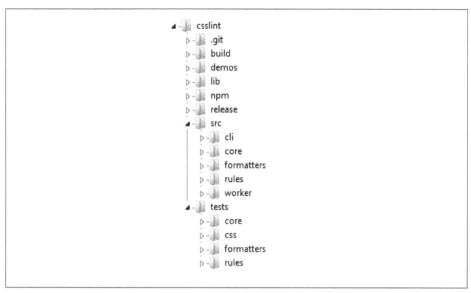

Figure 13-1. CSS Lint directory structure

jQuery (*https://github.com/jquery/jquery*) uses a form of this layout as well. The only difference is that jQuery puts all of its source files directly into the *src* directory rather than having subdirectories for each. Subdirectories are reserved for extensions and resources for the core features. The *test* directory then contains files with the same name as the source file it's testing. So *src/ajax.js* is tested by *test/ajax.js* (see Figure 13-2).

Dojo (*https://github.com/dojo/dojo*) uses a form similar to jQuery. The big difference with Dojo is that there is no top-level *src* directory. Instead, the top level contains source files as well as subdirectories for extensions and resources for core features. There is a top-level *tests* directory that mirrors the layout of the top-level directory itself, so *date.js* is tested by *tests/date.js* (see Figure 13-3).

YUI 3 (*https://github.com/yui/yui3*) uses a modification of the original layout. Each subdirectory of *src* represents a single YUI module, and each module has at least four subdirectories:

docs
    For documentation

js
    For JavaScript source files

meta
    For module metadata

tests
    For module tests

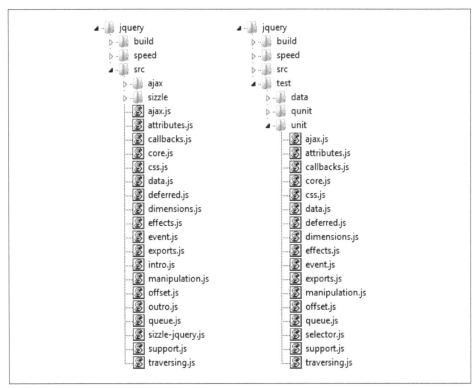

Figure 13-2. jQuery directory structure

Tests in YUI may be HTML files or JavaScript files, so exactly what's contained in *tests* varies from module to module. Generally, there is at least one file named the same as the source file, so *js/arraysort.js* is tested by *tests/arraysort.html* or *tests/arraysort.js*. See Figure 13-4.

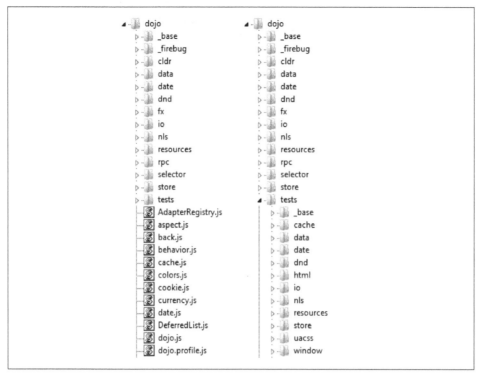

Figure 13-3. Dojo directory structure

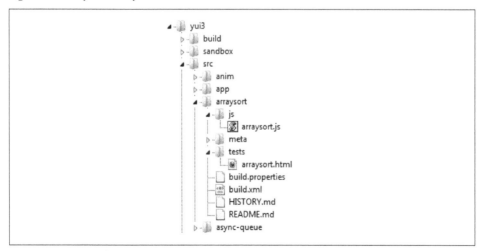

Figure 13-4. YUI 3 directory structure

Exactly which style of layout you choose will be largely based on your development and build process. It should be optimized to limit build time and make it easy for developers to know where new files should go.

CHAPTER 14

Ant

The choice of a build tool is usually based on the tools familiar to the developers who will be using it. My personal favorite tool for JavaScript build systems is Ant (*http://ant .apache.org*). Ant was originally created as a build tool for Java projects, but its easy XML syntax and built-in tasks make it an excellent choice for JavaScript as well. In an informal survey I conducted prior to writing this book, Ant was by far the most frequently cited build tool used for JavaScript, despite the recent introduction of newer build tools. If you find that Ant doesn't quite work for you, several alternatives are listed in Appendix B.

This book focuses on JavaScript build systems using Ant, but all of the tools and techniques discussed can be applied to other build systems as well.

Installation

Ant requires Java to run, so make sure that you have Java installed on your system. If you're using Mac OS X, then Ant is already installed by default; for Ubuntu, run *sudo apt-get install ant* to install Ant. For other operating systems, following the instructions at *http://ant.apache.org/manual/install.html*.

The Build File

The main build file for Ant is *build.xml*. When Ant runs on the command line, it looks for this file in the current directory, so it's best to place *build.xml* in the root directory of your project. You needn't keep all of the build-related information in this file, but *build.xml* must be present for Ant to work.

As you might expect, *build.xml* is an XML file containing instructions on how to perform the build. There are three basic parts of an Ant build system:

Task
A single step in the process such as running a program or copying a file

Target
A named grouping of tasks into sequential order

Project
A named container for all targets

Each part of the build system is represented by an XML element. Here's a sample *build.xml* file:

```
<project name="maintainablejs" default="hello">

    <target name="hello">
        <echo>Hello world!</echo>
    </target>

</project>
```

Every *build.xml* file begins with a `<project>` element representing the overall project. The `name` attribute is required and uniquely identifies this project. The `default` attribute specifies the default target to execute if no target is explicitly provided.

This file contains a single target, represented by the `<target>` element. The `name` attribute is also required here. The `<echo>` element represents the echo task, which outputs the enclosed text to the console. You can have any number of tasks in a target and any number of targets in a project.

 It's a standard practice to define targets as atomically as possible so they can be combined in any number of ways. Think of targets like you would functions, as a logical grouping of repeated tasks.

Running the Build

Once you have a *build.xml* file, open a command prompt in that directory and type:

```
ant
```

By default, Ant will read the *build.xml* file and `default` attribute of `<project>` to determine which target to execute. If you were to run `ant` with the *build.xml* file from the previous example, it would execute the `hello` target. You can optionally specify which target to run right on the command line:

```
ant hello
```

When the target name is specified on the command line, Ant no longer uses the default target.

In both cases, you'll see console output that looks like this:

```
Buildfile: /home/nicholas/tmp/build.xml

hello:
    [echo] Hello world!

BUILD SUCCESSFUL
Total time: 0 seconds
```

The output always shows you the build file being used as the first line. After that, you'll see the target being executed followed by a list of tasks being executed. The task name is enclosed in square braces; any output is displayed to the right. You will also see a message in capital letters indicating whether the build was successful, followed by the amount of time the build took. These items are all helpful in determining the cause of build errors.

Target Dependencies

Each target may optionally be specified with dependencies—other targets that must be run and must succeed before the current target is executed. Dependencies are specified using the depends attribute, which is a comma-separated ordered list of targets to execute first. Here's an example:

```
<project name="maintainablejs" default="hello">

    <target name="hello">
        <echo>Hello world!</echo>
    </target>

    <target name="goodbye" depends="hello">
        <echo>Goodbye!</echo>
    </target>

</project>
```

In this *build.xml* file, the target goodbye has a dependency on the target hello. Thus, running *ant goodbye* results in the following output:

```
Buildfile: /home/nicholas/tmp/build.xml

hello:
    [echo] Hello world!

goodbye:
    [echo] Goodbye!

BUILD SUCCESSFUL
Total time: 0 seconds
```

You can tell from the output that the hello target was executed before the goodbye target, and that both succeeded.

In most build files, there are a small number of targets that you'll use frequently. The majority of targets are single steps that are designed to be used by rollup targets that execute multiple targets in a specific order.

Properties

Ant properties are similar to variables in JavaScript, as they are generic containers for data that can be changed and manipulated throughout execution of the build script. A property is defined using the <property> element:

```
<project name="maintainablejs">

    <property name="version" value="0.1.0" />

</project>
```

Each <property> element requires name and value attributes. You can later reference the property by using ${version}, such as:

```
Version is ${version}
```

When this Ant script is executed, the output is:

```
Buildfile: /home/nicholas/tmp/build.xml

version:
     [echo] Version is 0.1.0

BUILD SUCCESSFUL
Total time: 0 seconds
```

The special ${} syntax is used any time you want to insert a property value into task.

Properties can also be defined in a Java properties files and loaded directly into Ant. For instance, suppose you have a properties file named *build.properties* containing the following:

```
version = 0.1.0
copyright = Copyright 2012 Nicholas C. Zakas. All rights reserved.
```

You can import these properties into the Ant script by using the <loadproperties> element and specifying the filename with the srcfile attribute:

```
<?xml version="1.0" encoding="UTF-8"?>

<project name="maintainablejs" default="version">

    <property name="version" value="0.1.0" />

    <target name="version">
        <echo>Version is ${version}</echo>
    </target>

</project>
```

Properties loaded using `<loadproperties>` are accessible in the same manner as those defined explicitly within *build.xml*. For a large number of properties, or properties that need to be shared among multiple Ant scripts, it's best to have them in a separate Java properties file.

At a minimum, it's best to have several properties declared that can be used throughout your project, such as:

`src.dir`
> The root source code location

`build.dir`
> Where the built files should end up

`lib.dir`
> Location of dependencies

Throughout the rest of this book, you'll see these properties used in Ant tasks. Be sure to define them appropriately in your project.

Buildr

Buildr (*https://github.com/nzakas/buildr*) is a project that seeks to collect common frontend-related Ant tasks with easier syntax. A wide range of tools is available for working with JavaScript files, but they all work a bit differently. Buildr wraps all of these different tools in tasks that can be used in your Ant scripts.

To use Buildr, you must first get a copy of the source. Once you have the directory structure on your computer, you can import all of the tasks with this command:

```
<import file="/path/to/buildr/buildr.xml"/>
```

This command allows your *build.xml* file to make use of all the custom tasks defined in Buildr. The following chapters show you both how to create Ant tasks from scratch as well as how to use the Buildr tasks.

CHAPTER 15

Validation

Because JavaScript isn't compiled before being deployed, web developers don't have the extra compilation step to identify errors. JavaScript code validators partly fill this void by performing static analysis on your JavaScript code. You were introduced to JSLint and JSHint earlier in this book. In this chapter, you'll learn how to incorporate JSHint into your build system to automatically analyze and verify your JavaScript code.

 JSHint is used in this chapter, because it comes with a prebuilt command-line file suitable for running with Rhino. JSLint, as of the time of this writing, doesn't have a prebuilt command-line file, though some third parties have written utilities including command-line controls for JSLint.

Finding Files

The first step in validating files is to locate the files. There are two different tasks for this purpose: `<fileset>` and `<filelist>`. The `<fileset>` task is used when you want to include a large number of files based on a pattern. Specify the `dir` attribute as the directory to look in and then `includes` with a filename pattern, such as:

```
<fileset dir="./src" includes="**/*.js" />
```

This fileset includes all JavaScript files contained in the *src* directory. You can optionally specify some file patterns to exclude as well:

```
<fileset dir="./src" includes="**/*.js" excludes="**/*-test.js />
```

This fileset includes all JavaScript files except the ones that end with *-test.js*. This is a common practice for excluding unit test files that are contained in the same directories as the source files.

The `<filelist>` task works similarly except that you must explicitly list the files to include. This task is best used when you want to retrieve references to a specific set of files. The `<fileset>` element also expects a `dir` for the directory. The `files` attribute contains a comma-separated list of files. For example:

```
<filelist dir="./src" files="core/core.js" />
```

In practice, you'll end up using `<fileset>` more frequently than `<filelist>`, as it's far more likely that you'll be dealing with large groups of files rather than specific, named files.

The Task

The `<apply>` task is used to execute command-line utilities on a collection of files from within an Ant target. Because JSHint is written in JavaScript, you'll need to use the Rhino command-line JavaScript engine to execute it. Download the latest Rhino release from *http://www.mozilla.org/rhino* and place the *js.jar* file in your dependencies folder (*lib.dir*).

To run JSHint on the command line, type the following:

```
java -jar js.jar jshint.js [options] [list of files]
```

For example:

```
java -jar js.jar jshint.js curly=true,noempty-true core/core.js
```

The `<apply>` task allows you to recreate command-line entires using the `<arg>` element. There are two ways to use `<arg>`: by specifying the `path` attribute for file or directory references, or by specifying the `line` attribute for plain text. You can break down the command-line format into the following pieces:

java
> The program to execute, specified by the `executable` attribute of `<apply>`

-jar
> An option for `java`, represented by the `line` attribute of `<arg>`

jshint.js
> The main JSHint file, represented by the `path` attribute of `<arg>`

curly=true,noempty-true
> The options, represented by the `line` attribute of `<arg>`

core/core.js
> The file to validate, represented by the `path` attribute of `<arg>`

Given that, you can quickly create an Ant skeleton for this utility:

```
<target name="validate">
  <apply executable="java">
    <arg line="-jar"/>
    <arg path="js.jar"/>
    <arg path="jshint.js" />
    <arg
      line="curly=true,forin=true,latedef=true,noempty=true,undef=true,rhino=false"
```

```
       />
       <arg path="core/core.js"/>
     </apply>
   </target>
```

Although this approach works, you should really run JSHint on a collection of Java-Script files rather than on a single one. The `<apply>` task makes this step easy by allowing you to specify a `<fileset>` and then include it in a particular spot on the command line by using the `<srcfile>` element. For example, the following target validates all Java-Script files in the source directory:

```
   <target name="validate">
     <apply executable="java">
       <fileset dir="${src.dir}" includes="**/*.js" />
       <arg line="-jar"/>
       <arg path="js.jar"/>
       <arg path="jshint.js" />
       <arg
        line="curly=true,forin=true,latedef=true,noempty=true,undef=true,rhino=false"
       />
       <srcfile/>
     </apply>
   </target>
```

This Ant target now executes JSHint on every file specified by the `<fileset>` element. You can run the target via:

```
   ant validate
```

Improving the Target

Although the `validate` target works well, there are some improvements that can be made. First, the current version runs JSHint once on each file. So if there are three JavaScript files, it's the equivalent of running this:

```
   java -jar js.jar jshint.js curly=true,noempty-true first.js
   java -jar js.jar jshint.js curly=true,noempty-true second.js
   java -jar js.jar jshint.js curly=true,noempty-true third.js
```

There is some overhead when running `java`, specifically the creation and destruction of the Java Virtual Machine (JVM). This task adds a significant amount of time to the target.

The JSHint command-line script actually accepts multiple files, so it's perfectly capable of using one JVM to check every file. Fortunately, the `<apply>` task makes it easy to pass in all of the filenames. You just need to set the `parallel` attribute to `"true"`:

```
   <target name="validate">
     <apply executable="java" parallel="true">
       <fileset dir="${src.dir}" includes="**/*.js" />
       <arg line="-jar"/>
       <arg path="js.jar"/>
       <arg path="jshint.js" />
```

```
      <arg
       line="curly=true,forin=true,latedef=true,noempty=true,undef=true,rhino=false"
      />
      <srcfile/>
    </apply>
  </target>
```

By adding one attribute, the `validate` target now passes all of the files onto the command line at once (separated by spaces). Doing so allows JSHint to read and validate all files with just one JVM and dramatically improves the target speed.

The last addition to the `validate` target is to have the build fail if validation fails. It's usually a good idea to add this step, because it ensures that developers are aware of the problem. The current version of the `validate` target will output validation failures to the command line, but any other task that follows will continue to execute, potentially causing the failure messages to scroll off screen.

You can force `<apply>` to fail the build by setting the `failonerror` property to "true":

```
  <target name="validate">
    <apply executable="java" failonerror="true" parallel="true">
      <fileset dir="${src.dir}" includes="**/*.js" />
      <arg line="-jar"/>
      <arg path="js.jar"/>
      <arg path="jshint.js" />
      <arg
       line="curly=true,forin=true,latedef=true,noempty=true,undef=true,rhino=false"
      />
      <srcfile/>
    </apply>
  </target>
```

This version of the `validate` target will fail the build when an error occurs during execution of `<apply>`. An error is any nonzero exit code returned from the executable. Because JSHint returns 1 when a validation error occurs, it will cause the build to fail.

Other Improvements

The last step in improving the `validate` task is to externalize three pieces of data:

- The location of *js.jar*
- The location of *jshint.js*
- The command-line options

As these may change in the future, it's best to represent them as properties and include them in your properties file or at the top of your *build.xml* file. Here's an example properties file:

```
  src.dir = ./src
  lib.dir = ./lib

  rhino = ${lib.dir}/js.jar
```

```
jshint = ${lib.dir}/jshint.js

jshint.options = curly=true,forin=true,latedef=true,noempty=true,undef=true\
,rhino=false
```

You can then reference the properties from the `validate` target:

```
<target name="validate">
    <apply executable="java" failonerror="true" parallel="true">
        <fileset dir="${src.dir}" includes="**/*.js" />
        <arg line="-jar"/>
        <arg path="${rhino}"/>
        <arg path="${jshint}" />
        <arg line="${jshint.options}" />
        <srcfile/>
    </apply>
</target>
```

With this change, you're easily able to update the location of files and JSHint options without needing to go back into the target.

Buildr Task

Buildr has a `<jshint>` task that abstracts away a lot of the configuration necessary to run JSHint. After importing the *buildr.xml* file as mentioned in the previous chapter, use the `<jshint>` task by passing in any number of `<fileset>` elements:

```
<target name="validate">
    <jshint>
        <fileset dir="${src.dir}" includes="**/*.js" />
    </jshint>
</target>
```

You can also change the default options by using the `options` attribute:

```
<target name="validate">
    <jshint options="${jshint.options}">
        <fileset dir="${src.dir}" includes="**/*.js" />
    </jshint>
</target>
```

The end result is exactly the same as using the target from the previous section.

CHAPTER 16

Concatenation and Baking

If you've properly set up your JavaScript files to contain one object per file, then it's likely you have dozens of JavaScript files. Before deploying to production, it's best to concatenate the files so there are fewer HTTP requests on the page. Exactly how many files and which files should be concatenated with which is a project-specific decision. In any case, Ant provides an easy way to concatenate multiple files.

The Task

The `<concat>` task is one of the simplest in Ant. You simply specify a `destfile` attribute containing the destination filename and then include as many `<fileset>` and `<file list>` elements as you want. At it's simplest, you can have a target such as:

```
<target name="concatenate">

    <concat destfile="${build.dir}/build.js">
        <fileset dir="${src.dir}" includes="**/*.js" />
    </concat>

</target>
```

This target concatenates all JavaScript files in the source directory into a single file called *build.js* in the build directory. Keep in mind that the files are concatenated in the order in which they appear on the filesystem (alphabetically). If you want a more specific ordering, you'll need to specify it explicitly, such as:

```
<target name="concatenate">

    <concat destfile="${build.dir}/build.js">
        <filelist dir="${src.dir}" files="first.js,second.js" />
        <fileset dir="${src.dir}" includes="**/*.js" excludes="first.js,second.js"/>
    </concat>

</target>
```

This version of the target ensures that *first.js* is the first file added to the final file and *second.js* comes right after that. Remember, you can use any number of `<fileset>` and `<filelist>` elements, so you can concatenate in any order you can imagine.

 Even though it's possible to create complex concatenation schemes using Ant, it's best to limit the special cases. Keeping filenames out of your build script is a good idea for maintainability. Try to use `<fileset>` elements whenever possible.

Line Endings

Concatenating files together comes with a series of challenges. One of the trickiest issues is dealing with the last line of a file. If a file doesn't have a newline character on its last line, then concatenating that file with another may result in broken syntax. By setting `fixlastline` attribute to `"yes"`, the `<concat>` task will automatically add a newline character to the last line if one doesn't already exist:

```
<target name="concatenate">

    <concat destfile="${build.dir}/build.js" fixlastline="yes">
        <filelist dir="${src.dir}" files="first.js,second.js" />
        <fileset dir="${src.dir}" includes="**/*.js" excludes="first.js,second.js"/>
    </concat>

</target>
```

It's a good idea to always set `fixlastline` to `"yes"` for JavaScript, as newlines are valid end-of-statement tokens.

Fixing the last line is useful, but how do you know which end-of-line marker is used? If your source files are being edited by people on different operating systems, you may want to ensure consistency in the built files. The `<concat>` task has an optional `eol` attribute that specifies which end-of-line markers to use. The default value is the default for the system (`"crlf"` for Windows, `"lf"` for Unix, and `"cr"` for Mac OS X). You can choose any one of these values, and all of the line endings in the concatenated file will automatically be switched to that format:

```
<target name="concatenate">

    <concat destfile="${build.dir}/build.js" fixlastline="yes" eol="lf">
        <filelist dir="${src.dir}" files="first.js,second.js" />
        <fileset dir="${src.dir}" includes="**/*.js" excludes="first.js,second.js"/>
    </concat>

</target>
```

This target changes all end-of-line markers to Unix style, which is the recommended format for JavaScript files, as it has the greatest cross-platform compatibility (and because most web servers run on a Unix variant).

Headers and Footers

The `<concat>` task also has the handy ability to prepend and append plain text to the resulting file. This capability allows you to insert pieces of information into the file that you might otherwise not have available. For instance, I tend to insert the build time into files so I can more easily track down errors. To do so, I start by defining a `<tstamp>` element at the top of the file:

```
<tstamp>
  <format property="build.time"
          pattern="MMMM d, yyyy hh:mm:ss"
          locale="en,US"/>
</tstamp>
```

This code creates a new timestamp when the *build.xml* file is executed by Ant. The resulting date string is stored in a property named `build.time`. The `pattern` attribute is a date-time formatting string. I can then use the `<header>` element to add this information into the built file:

```
<target name="concatenate">

    <concat destfile="${build.dir}/build.js" fixlastline="yes" eol="lf">
        <header>/* Build Time: ${build.time} */</header>
        <filelist dir="${src.dir}" files="first.js,second.js" />
        <fileset dir="${src.dir}" includes="**/*.js" excludes="first.js,second.js"/>
    </concat>

</target>
```

This new version of the `concatenate` target inserts a comment at the top of the file containing the build time. The resulting first line of the file has this format:

```
/* Build Time: May 25, 2012 03:20:45 */
```

There is also a `<footer>` element that can be used to add additional text at the bottom of the file. For example, this version of `concatenate` puts the build time at the bottom:

```
<target name="concatenate">

    <concat destfile="${build.dir}/build.js" fixlastline="yes" eol="lf">
        <filelist dir="${src.dir}" files="first.js,second.js" />
        <fileset dir="${src.dir}" includes="**/*.js" excludes="first.js,second.js"/>
        <footer>/* Build Time: ${build.time} */</footer>
    </concat>

</target>
```

You can use both `<header>` and `<footer>` at the same time or just one at a time.

Baking Files

Baking refers to the final touches you put into files before considering them ready for deployment. A lot of times, this step involves either adding additional text into a file or replacing existing text with something else. Inserting the build time, as in the previous example, is a type of baking. Other common tasks are automatically including license information and inserting version information. Both can be done very easily using Ant.

Many projects have a license file included somewhere in source control. The license file is separate because it may change independently of the code. It's useful to automatically insert the license information at the top of files before pushing them to production. You could potentially insert the license file using a `<filelist>` element, but that would mean that the license file must be in a property comment format for Java-Script. It's much easier to let the license file be plain text and add the comments around it. You can load text from any file using the `<loadfile>` task:

```
<loadfile property="license" srcfile="license.txt" />
```

This code loads text from *license.txt* and stores it in a property named `license`. Once it's in a property, you can use the `<header>` element to insert the text as a comment:

```
<target name="concatenate">

    <loadfile property="license" srcfile="license.txt" />

    <concat destfile="${build.dir}/build.js" fixlastline="yes" eol="lf">
        <header trimleading="yes">/*!
${license}
*/
/* Build time: ${build.time} */
        </header>
        <filelist dir="${src.dir}" files="first.js,second.js" />
        <fileset dir="${src.dir}" includes="**/*.js" excludes="first.js,second.js"/>
    </concat>

</target>
```

The license is inserted with a multiline JavaScript comment that has an exclamation point as the first character, which tells code minifiers (see Chapter 17) that the comment is important and should not be removed. The `<header>` element also has `trimleading` set to `"yes"`. This attribute specifies that leading white space on each line inside of `<header>` should be removed. That way, all text is aligned at the first column in the final file.

The other part of baking, replacing some text within files, is accomplished quite easily using the `<replaceregexp>` task. This task systematically goes through any number of files and uses regular expressions to replace values. As an example, I tend to use the token `@VERSION@` in my source files to indicate where the version number should be inserted. For instance, you might have this in a JavaScript file:

```
var MyProject = {
    version: "@VERSION@"
};
```

You can replace @VERSION@ with an actual version number using the following:

```
<replaceregexp match="@VERSION@" replace="${version}" flags="g" byline="true">
    <fileset dir="${build.dir}" includes="**/*"/>
</replaceregexp>
```

The `<replaceregexp>` task takes the regular expression from the `match` attribute and replaces it with the text in the `replace` attribute. Regular expression flags such as `g`, `i`, and `m` are specified using the `flags` attribute, and `byline` indicates whether the regular expression should match just a single line. You then specify any number of files in which this replacement should be made.

Because `<replaceregexp>` doesn't create new files, be sure to run it on the built files, as in the following example:

```
<target name="concatenate">

    <concat destfile="${build.dir}/build.js" fixlastline="yes" eol="lf">
        <filelist dir="${src.dir}" files="first.js,second.js" />
        <fileset dir="${src.dir}" includes="**/*.js" excludes="first.js,second.js"/>
        <footer>/* Build Time: ${build.time} */</footer>
    </concat>

    <replaceregexp match="@VERSION@" replace="${version}" flags="g" byline="true">
        <fileset dir="${build.dir}" includes="**/*"/>
    </replaceregexp>

</target>
```

This code replaces all instances of @VERSION@ in all built files with the `version` property. Although the replacement takes place in the `concatenate` target here, you may also want to have a separate target for baking, such as:

```
<target name="bake">

    <replaceregexp match="@VERSION@" replace="${version}" flags="g" byline="true">
        <fileset dir="${build.dir}" includes="**/*"/>
    </replaceregexp>

</target>
```

Separating out the baking step makes sense when it doesn't involve the `<concat>` task and may not always be done as part of the build process.

CHAPTER 17

Minification and Compression

Once you have your built files validated, concatenated, and baked, it's time to make those files as small as possible. This step is accomplished with two processes: minification and compression. Minification is the process of eliminating unnecessary white space, removing comments, and performing some processing on the files to make them as small as possible. Compression uses a specific compression method, such as `gzip`, to shrink the file even further. The difference between a minified file and a compressed file is that minified files are still just plain text and can be edited and loaded as usual (albeit with a bit of trouble, because all formatting is removed), whereas compressed files are unreadable and must be decompressed to be usable in a web page. Today's browsers automatically decompress any compressed files they receive with a `Content-Encoding: gzip` header in the response.

Minification

Minifying a JavaScript file isn't very complicated, but mistakes or invalid syntax can result if you use an unsafe process. For this reason, it's best to use a minifier that actually parses the JavaScript before making changes. Parsers know what valid syntax is and can more easily create valid syntax. The three most popular parsing minifiers are:

YUI Compressor

Often credited with popularizing parser-based minifiers instead of the regular expression-based minifiers. YUI Compressor was first written by Julien Lecomte (and is now maintained by the YUI team); it removes comments and extra white space and replaces local variable names with single- or double-character names to save even more space. YUI Compressor considers syntax and runtime safety as its highest priority, so it turns off variable replacement in cases in which errors might occur (such as using `eval()` or `with`). Download from *http://yuilibrary.com/projects/yui compressor/*.

Closure Compiler

A parser-based minifier that tries to make your code as small as possible. The Closure Compiler is written and maintained by Google engineers; it removes comments and extra white space and performs variable replacement, but also inspects your code for ways to optimize. For instance, it can detect that a function isn't used and simply remove it. It can also detect that a function is used only once and put it inline. For this reason, Closure Compiler works best when used on all of your JavaScript code at once. Download from *http://code.google.com/closure/compiler/*.

UglifyJS

Credited with being the first Node.js-based JavaScript minifier, UglifyJS is written in JavaScript using a JavaScript-based parser. Written by Mihai Bazon, UglifyJS removes comments and extra white space, replaces variable names, combines var statements, and performs other optimizations along the way. Download from *https://github.com/mishoo/UglifyJS* or install using npm.

Exactly which minifier to use is a matter of preference. Some prefer YUI Compressor because of its focus on ensuring that the resulting code doesn't contain errors and its simple optimizations. Others prefer Closure Compiler because it tends to produce files that are smaller than YUI Compressor. Still others prefer UglifyJS because it doesn't rely on Java and produces fewer syntax errors than Closure Compiler while also producing the smallest possible result.

Minifying with YUI Compressor

YUI Compressor ships as an executable JAR file that should be placed in your project's dependencies folder (in this example, this folder is referred to as *lib.dir*). There are several command-line options, but the most important to know are:

--disable-optimizations

Turns off micro optimizations such as changing obj["prop"] to obj.prop

--line-break <column>

Specifies to break lines at the given column rather than creating a single line of output

--nomunge

Turns off local variable name replacement

--preserve-semi

Turns off removal of unnecessary semicolons

Once you decide which options to use, place them in a Java properties file, as in the following example:

```
src.dir = ./src
lib.dir = ./lib

yuicompressor = ${lib.dir}/yuicompressor.jar

yuicompressor.options = --preserve-semi
```

Next, create a target for minification. As with validation, it's helpful to look at the command-line syntax first. To run YUI Compressor on the command line, type the following:

```
java -jar yuicompressor.jar [options] [file] -o [outputfile]
```

For example:

```
java -jar yuicompressor.jar --preserve-semi core/core.js -o core/core-min.js
```

This command runs YUI Compressor on *core/core.js* and outputs the result to *core/core-min.js*. Appending *-min* to the filename is a common practice when minifying files, so the target does that as well. The `<apply>` task is once again the one to use, and here's the target:

```
<target name="minify">

    <apply executable="java" failonerror="true">

        <fileset dir="${build.dir}" includes="*.js"/>
        <mapper type="glob" from="*.js" to="${build.dir}/*-min.js"/>

        <arg line="-jar"/>
        <arg path="${yuicompressor}"/>
        <arg line="${yuicompressor.options}"/>
        <srcfile/>

        <arg line="-o"/>
        <targetfile/>
    </apply>

</target>
```

This target is very similar to the `validate` target from earlier in the book. It starts by specifying the executable as `java` and then indicates that the command should be run on all JavaScript files in the build directory. These files get ready one by one and are put in the place of `<srcfile/>`. The next line uses the `<mapper>` task to translate filenames. It takes any `<srcfile/>` and appends *-min* to the filename. So *core.js* becomes *core-min.js*, and this value is used in place of the `<targetfile/>` element. The rest of the `<arg>` elements are self-explanatory.

The `minify` task is designed to be used after you've built files into the build directory but can easily be modified to run in any directory.

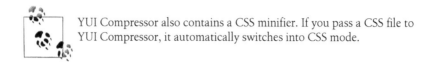

YUI Compressor also contains a CSS minifier. If you pass a CSS file to YUI Compressor, it automatically switches into CSS mode.

Buildr has a `<yuicompressor>` task that encapsulates all of this functionality. There are attributes to enable each command-line option (the attribute name is the same as the command-line option without the leading --) plus a required `outputdir` attribute that indicates where the minified files should be placed. Here's an example:

```
<target name="minify">
    <yuicompressor outputdir="${build.dir}" preserve-semi="true">
        <fileset dir="${build.dir}" includes="*.js" />
    </yuicompressor>
</target>
```

The `<yuicompressor>` task automatically adds the *-min* suffix to all files it creates. You can include one or more elements to minify everything at once.

Minifying with Closure Compiler

The Closure Compiler is also an executable JAR file that needs to be placed in the dependencies folder. The Closure Compiler has significantly more command-line options than the YUI Compressor, many of which are used only by those working directly with the Closure JavaScript library. The most important option is `--compilation_level`, which determines how much processing is done on the JavaScript file. The options are:

WHITESPACE_ONLY
> Removes only unnecessary white space and comments. Other optimizations are turned off.

SIMPLE_OPTIMIZATIONS
> The default setting for Closure Compiler. This setting removes unnecessary white space and comments while also renaming local variables to shorter names. The renaming happens even in the presence of `eval()` and `with`, so it may cause runtime errors if either is present.

ADVANCED_OPTIMIZATIONS
> Every optimization possible is done on the code. Use with caution, as this can introduce runtime or syntax errors.

Once you decide which options to use, place them in a Java properties file, such as:

```
src.dir = ./src
lib.dir = ./lib

closure = ${lib.dir}/compiler.jar

closure.options = --compilation_level SIMPLE_OPTIMIZATIONS
```

To run Closure Compiler on the command line, type the following:

```
java -jar compiler.jar [options] --js [file] --js_output_file [outputfile]
```

For example:

```
java -jar compiler.jar --compilation_level SIMPLE_OPTIMIZATIONS --js core/core.js
    --js_output_file core/core-min.js
```

This command runs Closure Compiler on *core/core.js* and outputs the result to *core/core-min.js*. The Ant target is basically the same as the one used with YUI Compressor:

```
<target name="minify">

    <apply executable="java" failonerror="true">

        <fileset dir="${build.dir}" includes="*.js"/>
        <mapper type="glob" from="*.js" to="${build.dir}/*-min.js"/>

        <arg line="-jar"/>
        <arg path="${closure}"/>
        <arg line="${closure.options}"/>

        <arg line="--js"/>
        <srcfile/>

        <arg line="--js_output_file"/>
        <targetfile/>
    </apply>

</target>
```

Aside from changing the JAR file path and command-line options, this target is virtually identical to the `minify` target. The end result is the same: every JavaScript file in the build directory is minified and output into a second file with the *-min* suffix.

Buildr has a `<closure>` task that encapsulates all of this functionality. You can set the compilation level using the `compilation-level` attribute. As with the `<yuicompressor>` task, the `outputdir` attribute is required and indicates where the minified files should be placed. Here's an example:

```
<target name="minify">
    <closure outputdir="${build.dir}" compilation-level="SIMPLE_OPTIMIZATIONS">
        <fileset dir="${build.dir}" includes="*.js" />
    </closure>
</target>
```

The `<closure>` task automatically adds the *-min* suffix to all files it creates. You can include one or more elements to minify everything at once.

Minifying with UglifyJS

UglifyJS is most commonly used on the command line through npm, the Node.js package manager. You must have both Node.js and npm installed first before you can install UglifyJS, which is done with this command:

```
sudo npm install -g uglify-js
```

The UglifyJS command-line interface also has a large number of options. However, the most commonly used are:

`--beautify`
: Beautifies the code instead of minifying it

`--no-mangle`
: Turns off function and variable name replacement

`--no-mangle-functions`
: Turns off only function name replacement

`--no-dead-code`
: Enables removal of unreachable code

The basic format of UglifyJS on the command line is:

```
uglifyjs [options] -o [outputfile] [file]
```

For example:

```
uglifyjs --no-mangle-functions -o core/core-min.js core/core.js
```

This command runs UglifyJS on *core/core.js* and outputs the result to *core/core-min.js*. It's important that the original file comes after all of the other options.

As with the other minifiers, it's best to put your preferred options into a properties file, as in:

```
src.dir = ./src
lib.dir = ./lib

uglifyjs = uglifyjs

uglifyjs.options = --no-mangle-functions
```

The Ant target for UglifyJS is a bit easier than the others, because it is a standalone executable. Instead of setting the `executable` attribute of `<apply>` to Java, set it to `uglifyjs`. Then pass the additional information as usual:

```
<target name="minify">

    <apply executable="uglifyjs" failonerror="true">

        <fileset dir="${build.dir}" includes="*.js"/>
        <mapper type="glob" from="*.js" to="${build.dir}/*-min.js"/>

        <arg line="${ugilfyjs.options}"/>
```

```
                <arg line="-o"/>
                <targetfile/>
                <srcfile/>
        </apply>

    </target>
```

The `minify` target is the same basic format as the other targets in this chapter and produces a similar result. All of the files in the build directory are minified and placed into files with the *-min* suffix.

Buildr has an `<uglifyjs>` task that makes using UglifyJS easier. Each of the command-line options is available as an attribute (without the leading `--`), and as with the other minification tasks, the `outputdir` attribute is required. Here's an example:

```
<target name="minify">
    <uglifyjs outputdir="${build.dir}" no-mangle-functions="true">
        <fileset dir="${build.dir}" includes="*.js" />
    </uglifyjs>
</target>
```

The `<uglifyjs>` task works in the same way as the others: *-min* is automatically added to minified filenames, and you can specify as many `<fileset>` elements as you'd like.

Compression

Minification of JavaScript files is the first step before deployment. The second is to compress the files to be as small as possible during transmission. The minifiers mentioned in this chapter don't perform compression on JavaScript (even YUI Compressor only performs minification). Compression usually happens later in the process, either at runtime using HTTP compression on the web server or during build time.

Runtime Compression

Most web servers are capable of performing runtime compression of files. In practice, such compression is typically done only for text-based files such as JavaScript, HTML, and CSS. Modern browsers all support HTTP compression and will send an HTTP header as part of a request indicating the types of compression supported. For example:

```
Accept-Encoding: gzip, deflate
```

When the server sees this HTTP header in a request, it knows the browser is capable of decompressing files that are compressed using either gzip or deflate. When the server sends the response, it sets a header indicating the type of compression used, such as:

```
Content-Encoding: gzip
```

This header tells the browser that the body of the response is gzipped and must be uncompressed before use.

Apache 2, one of the most popular web servers, has HTTP compression built in as the `mod_deflate` module. This module is enabled by default and automatically compresses JavaScript, HTML, CSS, and XML files. If you're using Apache 2, then you don't need to do any further configuration for compressing JavaScript files.

Nginx, another popular web server, also has HTTP compression built in using gzip. Compression is also enabled by default for JavaScript, HTML, CSS, and XML files. If you're using Nginx, then no further configuration is needed to enable compression for JavaScript.

 Internet Explorer 6 and earlier had problems with HTTP compression in certain situations. Apache 2 and Nginx allow you to turn off HTTP compression for these browsers if necessary. Since Microsoft began auto-upgrading everyone with Internet Explorer 6 to Internet Explorer 8 in 2012, this should no longer be much of a problem.

Build-Time Compression

You may choose to compress files during build time if you want to distribute the compressed file yourself without any server intervention. jQuery builds a gzipped version of the main JavaScript file and makes it available for download from *http://jquery .com*. Gzipping is the easiest way to perform compression at build time due to Ant's `<gzip>` task.

The `<gzip>` task works only on a single file. You specify the `src` attribute as the filename to compress and the `destfile` attribute as the output file. For example:

```
<gzip src="${build.dir}/build.js" destfile="${build.dir}/build.js.gz"/>
```

This task gzips the *build.js* file and outputs the result to *build.js.gz*. You can certainly use `<gzip>` in this manner if you only ever have one file to gzip. For example:

```
<target name="compress">

    <gzip src="${build.dir}/build.js" destfile="${build.dir}/build.js.gz"/>

</target>
```

In this case, the filenames should be stored in properties so they can be easily changed later.

A little bit of creativity is required to gzip multiple files without explicitly setting their filenames. Ant doesn't have a native way of looping over a list of files. However, it's possible to use JavaScript inside of Ant to provide this behavior.

The Ant `<script>` task allows you to write scripts in a number of languages, of which JavaScript is just one. To specify JavaScript as the language you're using, set the `language` attribute to `"javascript"`. After that, enclose the contents of the `<script>` element with CData delimiters such as this:

```
<script language="javascript"><![CDATA[

    // code here

]]></script>
```

Adding the CData delimiters ensures that you needn't worry about escaping characters within the script.

JavaScript inside of the `<script>` task executes in an environment similar to the default environment in Rhino. You have access to Java objects and can import more by using the `importPackage()` function. There is also a `project` object that refers to the overall project represented in *build.xml*. You can read properties using `project.getProperty()` and create new tasks using `project.createTask()`. Putting these pieces together, you can create a `compress` target that compresses all files in the build directory:

```
<target name="compress">

    <!-- store filenames in a property delimited by ; -->
    <pathconvert pathsep=";" property="compress.jsfiles">
        <fileset dir="${build.dir}" includes="*.js"/>
    </pathconvert>

    <script language="javascript"><![CDATA[

        importPackage(java.io);

        <!-- get the property and convert to an array-->
        var files = project.getProperty("compress.jsfiles").split(";"),
            gzip,
            i,
            len;

        for (i=0, len=files.length; i < len; i++) {

            // create new gzip task
            gzip = project.createTask("gzip");
            gzip.setSrc(new File(files[i]));
            gzip.setDestfile(new File(files[i].replace(".js", ".js.gz")));
            gzip.perform();
        }

    ]]> </script>
</target>
```

The first part of the `compress` target converts a `<fileset>` into a property. The property `compress.jsfiles` is filled with a string in which the filenames are separated by semicolons. Inside the `<script>` task, the first line imports the `java.io` package so that the `File` class is available. Next, the `compress.jsfiles` property is read and split with semicolons so that `files` is an array of filenames.

After that, a `for` loop is used to iterate over the filenames. For each filename, a new `<gzip>` task is created using `project.createTask("gzip")`. The `gzip` variable then contains a Java object representing the task. Each attribute has a method for setting its value and a method for getting its value, so `setSrc()` is used to set the `src` attribute and `setDestfile()` is used to set the `destfile` attribute. Both attributes represent files, so it's necessary to pass an instance of `File` instead of the filename. The output file is set to have a *.js.gz* extension by using the JavaScript `replace()` method on the filename. The last step is to call `perform()`, which actually executes the task.

This version of the `compress` target doesn't rely on knowing the filename ahead of time and is therefore better suited for general usage.

There is a Buildr `<gzipall>` task that allows you to compress multiple files:

```
<target name="compress">
    <gzipall>
        <fileset dir="${build.dir}" includes="*-min.js" />
    </gzipall>
</target>
```

Using `<gzipall>`, a gzipped file is created with a *.gz* appended to the filename.

If you intend to serve the compressed file yourself, you'll still need to configure the web server to send the `Content-Encoding: gzip` header so that the browser can use the file correctly.

CHAPTER 18

Documentation

All engineers would rather be writing code than documentation, which is precisely why tools that autogenerate documentation from code are so popular. The trend really began with Javadoc, the tool that automatically creates documentation for Java, and continued into other languages such as JavaScript.

There is a large (and growing) number of documentation generators that work with JavaScript. Some are general-purpose documentation generators that work with any language; others are JavaScript-specific. As with minifiers, the choice of documentation generator is more of a preference than anything else. This chapter covers a few popular choices; there are many more out there. See Appendix B for a full list of alternatives.

JSDoc Toolkit

JSDoc Toolkit (*http://code.google.com/p/jsdoc-toolkit/*) is perhaps the most commonly used JavaScript documentation generator. An evolution of the original JSDoc released in 2011, JSDoc Toolkit is used by Google and SproutCore and is often credited with starting the trend of writing JavaScript-specific documentation generators. It uses the same basic syntax as Javadoc, with special multiline comments indicating documentation information. For example:

```
/**
 * @namespace The main application object.
 */
var MyApplication = {

    /**
     * Adds two numbers together.
     * @param {int} num1 The first number.
     * @param {int} num2 The second number.
     * @returns {int} The sum of the two numbers.
     * @static
     */
    add: function (num1, num2) {
        return num1 + num2;
```

```
        }
    }
```

Any object for which there is no constructor to call is considered a namespace in JSDoc. So `MyApplication` is a namespace and is indicated as such by the `@namespace` tag followed by the description. The method `MyApplication.add()` has two parameters, specified by `@param` and followed by the expected data type, the parameter name, and the description. The method returns a result, so the `@return` tag indicates the expected data type and describes the return value. The `@static` tag indicates that the method doesn't require instantiation of an object to be used.

When JSDoc Toolkit processes JavaScript files, it looks both at the JavaScript code and at the documentation comments to create HTML-based documentation. For full syntax information, see *http://code.google.com/p/jsdoc-toolkit/w/list*.

JSDoc Toolkit is written almost entirely in JavaScript and uses a custom Rhino launcher JAR file (*jsrun.jar*) to execute:

```
java -jar jsrun.jar app/run.js [file]+ -t=[templates] -d=[directory] [options]
```

The *app/run.js* file is the main executable for JSDoc toolkit. You can pass in as many JavaScript files as you'd like to document. The `-t` flag specifies the templates to use (by default, you can use the ones that come with JSDoc Toolkit) and `-d` specifies the output directory. For example:

```
java -jar jsrun.jar app/run.js core/core.js -t=templates/jsdoc/ -d=./out
```

This command creates documentation for *core/core.js* using the templates in *templates/jsdoc/* and outputs the final HTML documentation to the *out* directory. Because you need to use the JSDoc Toolkit directory several times (for *jsrun.jar*, *app/run.js*, and the default templates), it's best to keep this information in properties, as in the following:

```
src.dir = ./src
lib.dir = ./lib

jsdoc.dir = ${lib.dir}/jsdoc-toolkit
jsdoc = ${jsdoc.dir}/jsrun.jar
jsdoc.run = ${jsdoc.dir}/app/run.js
jsdoc.templates = ${jsdoc.dir}/templates
jsdoc.output = ./docs
```

The target for generating documentation is as follows:

```
<target name="document">
    <apply executable="java" failonerror="true" parallel="true">
        <fileset dir="${src.dir}" includes="**/*.js" />
        <arg line="-jar"/>
        <arg path="${jsdoc}"/>
        <arg path="${jsdoc.run}" />
        <arg line="-t=${jsdoc.templates}" />
        <arg line="-d=${jsdoc.output}" />
        <srcfile/>
    </apply>
</target>
```

Because the built files have all comments stripped, the `document` target generates documentation on the source files instead. Similar to the `validate` target, the `<apply>` task has `parallel` set to `"true"` so that all of the files are passed on the command line at once. The rest are just `<arg>` elements specifying the different options. By default, the documentation is generated into a top-level *docs* directory, but you may want to change that location based on your directory structure.

The Buildr task for JSDoc is `<jsdoc>` and has a required `outputdir` attribute. There is also a `templates` attribute that is optional (if you don't want to use the default). For example:

```
<target name="document">
    <jsdoc outputdir="${jsdoc.output}">
        <fileset dir="${src.dir}" includes="**/*.js" />
    </jsdoc>
</target>
```

This target functions the same as the previous version but is a bit more obvious about what it's doing.

YUI Doc

The original version of YUI Doc was written in Python and was used by the YUI library for several years. More recently, a new JavaScript version was created that understands the same syntax. This is the tool that generates the documentation on *http://yuilibrary .com*. The syntax is very similar to JSDoc, as it is based off of Javadoc-style comments. The biggest difference is that YUI Doc requires you to name your properties and methods in the documentation comment, whereas JSDoc is able to infer the name from looking at the JavaScript code. For example:

```
/**
 * The main application object.
 * @class MyApplication
 * @static
 */
var MyApplication = {

    /**
     * Adds two numbers together.
     * @param {int} num1 The first number.
     * @param {int} num2 The second number.
     * @returns {int} The sum of the two numbers.
     * @method add
     */
    add: function (num1, num2) {
        return num1 + num2;
    }
}
```

In YUI Doc terms, `MyApplication` is a class even though it has no constructor. The class description is the first line, and `@class MyApplication` identifies the object as a class. Because there is no constructor, the `@static` tag indicates that `MyApplication` is an object and all of its methods are accessed statically. The `MyApplication.add()` method has syntax that's very similar to JSDoc, with the main difference being the `@method` tag indicating the method name.

YUI Doc is written in JavaScript and runs on Node.js. It can be installed using npm via:

```
sudo npm install -g yuidoc
```

The command line for YUI Doc is simpler than that of JSDoc:

```
yuidoc [options] [directory]+ -o [directory]
```

For example:

```
yuidoc ./src -o ./docs
```

This command recursively goes through the *src* directory and parses all JavaScript files it finds. The generated HTML documentation ends up in the *docs* directory. Even though there are command-line options for YUI Doc, they aren't necessary in order to get up and running. The properties for YUI Doc are simple:

```
src.dir = ./src
lib.dir = ./lib

yuidoc = yuidoc
yuidoc.output = ./docs
```

You may be wondering what the value of having `yuidoc = yuidoc` is, as it's redundant. It's always best to keep application paths as properties, because paths and filenames have a tendency to change over time. Even though these are identical now, there's no telling if this will remain true in the future. When things change, you want to be able to make a quick change to the properties file rather than going through the *build.xml* to find where the executable is set.

Because YUI Doc expects one or more directories to be passed in instead of files, the target becomes very simple when there's just one source directory:

```
<target name="document">
    <exec executable="yuidoc" failonerror="true">
        <arg path="${src.dir}"/>
        <arg line="-o" />
        <arg path="${yuidoc.output}"/>
    </exec>
</target>
```

This target uses `<exec>` instead of `<apply>`, because there is only a single directory being passed in. The `<exec>` task functions similarly to `<apply>`, except that it doesn't require a `<srcfile>` element. The `<arg>` elements construct the full command line.

The Buildr `<yuidoc>` task encapsulates this functionality and has two required attributes, `inputdir` and `outputdir`, to specify where the JavaScript files are and where the documentation should be generated, respectively. For example:

```
<target name="document">
    <yuidoc inputdir="${src.dir}" outputdir="${yuidoc.output}"/>
</target>
```

The `<yuidoc>` task assumes that you have YUI Doc installed already.

CHAPTER 19

Automated Testing

Testing JavaScript has long been a pain point for developers. You want to test JavaScript quickly and easily, but there are so many browsers to test. The first solution was manual testing across all browsers, which meant creating an HTML file and manually loading it in various browsers to ensure that it worked. Though functional, this approach was too slow for practical use.

The next wave of JavaScript testing focused on command-line testing by stubbing out the browser environment. Several attempts were made to get JavaScript testing on the command line using Rhino and a fake browser environment. Some companies even developed browser profiles that could be loaded in with the promise of cross-browser testing. The unfortunate reality was that these stubbed browser environments didn't do the job. Trying to recreate a truly unique environment by hand led to inconsistencies: your tests might pass in the "fake Firefox" but fail in the actual browser.

More recently, attempts have been made to use the actual browsers for testing. This approach typically involves using an HTML file to launch tests and then having an application load that file in the different browsers. Many of the tools mentioned in this chapter are still under development, but they all give you a good starting point for integrating browser-based JavaScript testing.

YUI Test Selenium Driver

YUI Test (*http://yuilibrary.com/projects/yuitest*) is the unit testing framework for the YUI Library. The most recent version of YUI Test is more than a simple testing library. In addition to removing dependencies on the core YUI library, YUI Test supports a suite of utilities to aid JavaScript testing. One of these tools is called the YUI Test Selenium Driver and is designed to work with Selenium to enable easy browser testing.

Selenium (*http://seleniumhq.com*) is a server that is capable of launching browsers and running commands inside of them. Originally intended for use by QA engineers writing functional tests, Selenium gained popularity for JavaScript testing due to the ease with which it interacts with browsers.

Setting Up a Selenium Server

The YUI Test Selenium Driver works with a Selenium server to run JavaScript tests on various browsers and return the results. The first step is to set up your Selenium server (if you don't already have one). Selenium is written in Java, so it can be run anywhere Java is installed. Download the latest Selenium server from *http://seleniumhq.org/down load/*.

To run your Selenium server, go to the directory containing the downloaded files and run:

```
java -jar selenium-server-standalone-x.y.z.jar
```

The server takes a few moments to set up and then is ready to receive commands.

Setting Up YUI Test Selenium Driver

There are three steps to setting up the YUI Test Selenium Driver:

1. Download the latest version of YUI Test.
2. Place *yuitest-selenium-driver.jar* in your dependencies directory.
3. Copy *selenium-java-client-driver.jar* from the YUI Test *lib* directory into your Java Runtime Environment (JRE)'s *lib/ext* directory.

With these steps completed, it's now possible to run tests using the YUI Test Selenium Driver.

Using the YUI Test Selenium Driver

The YUI Test Selenium Driver uses HTML files for testing. Even if your tests are in standalone JavaScript files, you must include them in an HTML file that automatically runs the tests upon page load. The following is an example test page:

```html
<!DOCTYPE html>
<html>
<head>
    <title>YUI Test</title>

    <!-- include YUI Test library -->
    <script src="yuitest.js"></script>

    <!-- include your test files -->
    <script src="tests1.js"></script>
    <script src="tests2.js"></script>
</head>
<body>
    <script>
        YUITest.TestRunner.run();
    </script>
</body>
</html>
```

Each of the JavaScript test files should add their tests to YUI Test via `YUITest.TestRun ner.add()`. That way, the tests can simply be run automatically once they're fully loaded.

Assuming this HTML file lives on a server as *http://www.example.com/tests.html*, you can then run the tests using the following command:

```
java -jar yuitest-selenium-driver.jar [options] [url]+
```

For example:

```
java -jar yuitest-selenium-driver.jar http://www.example.com/tests.html
```

This command runs the given file in Firefox (the default browser on Selenium) and assumes the Selenium server is running on `localhost:4444` (the default Selenium port). You can change the location of Selenium by adding some options:

```
java -jar yuitest-selenium-driver.jar --host testing.example.com
    --port 9000 http://www.example.com/tests.html
```

This command runs the given file in Firefox on the Selenium server at `testing.exam ple.com:9000`. You can also specify additional browsers using the Selenium IDs:

```
java -jar yuitest-selenium-driver.jar
    --browsers *firefox,*iexplore http://www.example.com/tests.html
```

This command runs the tests both in Firefox and in Internet Explorer. The `--browsers` option passes through these options directly to Selenium and must therefore specify valid Selenium browsers. An error occurs if a given browser isn't available on the specified Selenium server.

Although it's possible to pass test URLs on the command line, most developers use the test configuration XML file instead. The XML file has the following format:

```
<?xml version="1.0"?>
<yuitest>
    <tests base="http://www.example.com/tests/" timeout="10000">
        <url>test_core</url>
        <url timeout="30000">test_util</url>
        <url>test_ui</url>
    </tests>
</yuitest>
```

The `<tests>` element is used to specify a base path and default timeout value for each test. Then, each `<url>` element specifies the relative path to a test page. Tell the YUI Test Selenium Driver to use the XML file instead of the command line by specifying the `--tests` option:

```
java -jar yuitest-selenium-driver.jar --tests tests.xml
```

The YUI Test Selenium Driver then goes through each of the tests, runs them on each of the specified browsers, and returns all of the results.

There is an `--erroronfail` option that indicates the YUI Test Selenium Driver should exit with a nonzero code when a test fails. It's a good idea to specify this option so that the build will stop when a test fails rather than continue.

The Ant Target

To create the Ant target, start by specifying the key pieces of data in a properties file:

```
src.dir = ./src
lib.dir = ./lib
tests.dir = ./tests

yuitestselenium = ${lib.dir}/yuitest-selenium-driver.jar

yuitestselenium.host = testing.example.com
yuitestselenium.port = 4444
yuitestselenium.tests = ${tests.dir}/tests.xml
yuitestselenium.browsers = *firefox
```

The Ant target uses the `<exec>` task to run the YUI Test Selenium Driver and pass in the relevant information:

```
<target name="test">

    <exec executable="java" failonerror="true">
        <arg line="-jar"/>
        <arg path="${yuitestselenium}"/>
        <arg line="--host ${yuitestselenium.host}"/>
        <arg line="--port ${yuitestselenium.port}"/>
        <arg line="--browsers ${yuitestselenium.browsers}"/>
        <arg line="--tests ${yuitestselenium.tests}"/>
        <arg line="--erroronfail"/>
    </exec>

</target>
```

The `test` target will fail if the Selenium Server isn't running, or if a test times out, or if a specified browser doesn't exist. It's important to check all of these conditions before running tests.

The Buildr `<yuitest-selenium>` task encapsulates all of this functionality. The `-error onfail` flag is always passed in, and the other options are available as attributes:

```
<target name="test">

    <yuitest-selenium host="${yuitestselenium.host}"
        port="${yuitestselenium.port}" browsers="${yuitestselenium.browsers}"
        tests="${yuitestselenium.tests}"/>

</target>
```

The `tests` attribute is required for `<yuitest-selenium>`; all other attributes are optional.

Yeti

Yeti (*http://yuilibrary.com/projects/yeti*) is another tool designed to work with YUI Test. Unlike the YUI Test Selenium Driver, Yeti is a completely standalone solution written in JavaScript that runs on Node.js. Yeti requires you to have an HTML file that automatically executes your tests, so you can use the same HTML files that are used with the YUI Test Selenium Driver.

You can install Yeti via npm with:

```
sudo npm install -g yeti
```

Running Yeti is simply a matter of passing in the HTML file on the command line:

```
yeti test.html
```

This command runs all of the tests on Firefox or Safari by default (depending on platform) and outputs the result to the command line. If a Yeti server is running locally, then this command also runs tests on all connected browsers and reports all results.

Due to the simplicity of Yeti, the Ant target requires very little configuration in a properties file:

```
src.dir = ./src
lib.dir = ./lib
tests.dir = ./tests

yeti = yeti
```

And the Ant target itself is very straightforward as well:

```
<target name="test">

    <apply executable="yeti" failonerror="true" parallel="true">
        <fileset dir="${tests.dir}" includes="**/*.html" />
        <srcfile/>
    </apply>

</target>
```

The test target uses the <apply> task to pass all HTML files found in the *tests* directory to Yeti. The results are output on the screen, and the build will fail if there are errors.

The Buildr <yeti> task makes using Yeti even simpler:

```
<target name="test">

    <yeti>
        <fileset dir="${tests.dir}" includes="**/*.html" />
    </yeti>

</target>
```

Keep in mind that the <yeti> task requires you to have Yeti already installed on the computer that is executing the build script.

PhantomJS

PhantomJS (*http://www.phantomjs.org*) is a headless version of WebKit, the rendering engine that powers Safari and Chrome. As such, it acts very similarly to these browsers (though not exactly the same) and allows you to perform true browser testing without actually opening a browser. PhantomJS comes with scripts to run tests in two different JavaScript testing frameworks: Jasmine (*http://pivotal.github.com/jasmine/*) and QUnit (*http://docs.jquery.com/QUnit*).

PhantomJS isn't just a browser—it's also a scripting environment for that browser. The scripts to run Jasmine and QUnit are part of a suite of scripts that ships with PhantomJS. Both scripts require you to use the appropriate HTML page template for the framework being used.

Installation and Usage

If you're using Ubuntu, then you can install via **apt-get** using:

```
$ sudo add-apt-repository ppa:jerome-etienne/neoip
$ sudo apt-get update
$ sudo apt-get install phantomjs
```

If you're using Homebrew on Mac OS X, you can also install PhantomJS via the following command:

```
brew install phantomjs
```

For other platforms, download the latest executable for your platform from *http://code .google.com/p/phantomjs/downloads/list*. Place the entire PhantomJS directory in an easily accessible location (your dependencies directory or someplace else). The scripts to run Jasmine and QUnit tests are in the *examples* directory.

 If you installed using Homebrew or **apt-get**, then you'll need to download the files to run Jasmine and QUnit tests from the PhantomJS repository, as these are not included by default.

PhantomJS runs Jasmine and QUnit tests on the command line in the following format:

```
phantomjs [driver] [HTML file]
```

For example, to run QUnit:

```
phantomjs examples/run-qunit.js tests.html
```

And to run Jasmine:

```
phantomjs examples/run-jasmine.js tests.html
```

The results are output onto the command line.

The Ant Target

As with Yeti, the Ant target for PhantomJS is quite simple. There are just a few properties to keep track of:

```
src.dir = ./src
lib.dir = ./lib
tests.dir = ./tests

phantomjs = phantomjs
phantomjs.driver = ${lib.dir}/phantomjs/examples/run-qunit.js
phantomjs.tests = tests.html
```

Because the PhantomJS test runners support passing in only one file at a time, the Ant target uses <exec> instead of <apply>:

```
<target name="test">

    <exec executable="phantomjs" failonerror="true">
        <arg path="${phantomjs.driver}"/>
        <arg path="${tests.dir}/${phantomjs.tests}"/>
    </exec>

</target>
```

The test target just passes two paths to the executable and fails if there's an error.

The Buildr <phantomjs> task allows you to perform the same operation with a slightly different syntax:

```
<target name="test">

    <phantomjs driver="${phantomjs.driver}">
        <fileset dir="${tests.dir}" includes="*.html" />
    </phantomjs>

</target>
```

The driver attribute is required and specifies the PhantomJS driver to use for your tests. The <phantomjs> task expects one or more <fileset> elements to be present specifying the tests to run. Otherwise, it behaves the same as the previous test target.

JsTestDriver

JsTestDriver (*http://code.google.com/p/js-test-driver/*) is a command-line utility written by engineers at Google. Similar to Selenium and Yeti, JsTestDriver works with already installed browsers to run tests. JsTestDriver has its own JavaScript testing framework as well, so you must write tests using that library by default. There is a QUnit adapter to allow QUnit-based tests to be executed with JsTestDriver, and it's possible to write your own adapter if you so choose.

Installation and Usage

JsTestDriver is written in Java, so you must first download the latest JAR file and put it into your dependencies directory. JsTestDriver's most common mode is to run on a developer machine by manually connecting browsers to the JsTestDriver server. Configuration information, including which files to execute as tests, are included in a YAML file that looks like this:

```
server: http://localhost:4224

load:
    - tests/*.js
```

The first line indicates where the JsTestDriver server should be set up and the `load` section indicates which JavaScript files to load for testing.

For a build system, JsTestDriver offers a command that automatically starts and stops browsers all while collecting test results. The format is as follows:

```
java -jar JsTestDriver.jar --port [port] --browser [browsers] --config [file]
    --tests all --testOutput [directory]
```

For example:

```
java -jar JsTestDriver.jar --port 4224 --browser firefox,iexplore
    --config conf/conf.yml --tests all --testOutput ./results
```

This command runs all tests specified in *conf/conf.yml* on Firefox and Internet Explorer and outputs the results in *results*. The `--browsers` option requires the path to the browser executables, so this example assumes that both `firefox` and `iexplore` are executable without a full path.

The Ant Target

Creating a target for JsTestDriver requires keeping track of a few key pieces of information:

```
src.dir = ./src
lib.dir = ./lib
tests.dir = ./tests

jstestdriver = ${lib.dir}/JsTestDriver.jar
jstestdriver.port = 4224
jstestdriver.browser = firefox,iexplore
jstestdriver.config = conf/conf.yml
jstestdriver.output = ./results
```

The Ant target looks very similar to the one for YUI Test Selenium Driver:

```
<target name="test">

    <exec executable="java" failonerror="true">
        <arg line="-jar"/>
        <arg path="${jstestdriver}"/>
```

```
        <arg line="--port ${jstestdriver.port}"/>
        <arg line="--browser ${jstestdriver.browser}"/>
        <arg line="--conf"/>
        <arg path="${jstestdriver.config}"/>
        <arg line="--tests all"/>
        <arg line="--testOutput"/>
        <arg path="${jstestdriver.output}"/>
    </exec>

  </target>
```

As currently configured, this Ant target will run all tests specified in the configuration file on Firefox and Internet Explorer.

The Buildr `<jstestdriver>` task makes it simpler to use JsTestDriver. There are two required attributes: `outputdir` for the location of the results and `config` for the location of the configuration file. All other command-line options are present as attributes as well. The following is equivalent to the last example target:

```
<target name="test">

    <jstestdriver config="${jstestdriver.config}"
        outputdir="${jstestdriver.output}"
        tests="all" port="${jstestdriver.port}"
        browser="${jstestdriver.browser}"/>

</target>
```

CHAPTER 20

Putting It Together

The preceding chapters about the build system focused on creating small pieces of a build system, creating a library of utilities that could easily be put together later. This chapter focuses on assembling the system into an end-to-end solution for your Java-Script. For your final system, you may have more complex functionality and may choose to use a bundled set of tasks such as Buildr, but there are still some common pieces of functionality that all build systems have.

Missing Pieces

Before putting together the build system, there are a couple of small steps that are missing. The first is the creation of the *build* directory. As this directory is transient (and won't be checked in), the build system is responsible for its creation. The `<mkdir>` Ant task handles this easily:

```
<target name="init">
    <mkdir dir="${build.dir}"/>
</target>
```

The `init` target just does one thing: create the build directory so all the built files have a place to be put. It's possible that other tasks, such as `<concat>`, may end up making this directory if it doesn't already exist. However, it's best to explicitly state each step of the build process to ensure that reordering of tasks or targets doesn't cause errors.

The second missing piece is the cleanup of the *build* directory. In between builds, you want to remove all files and start over from scratch. The fastest way to do that is simply to delete the *build* directory using the `<delete>` task:

```
<target name="clean">
    <delete dir="${build.dir}"/>
</target>
```

The `clean` target removes the *build* directory so you're certain to get the latest files.

Planning the Build

To put the build system pieces together in the correct order, it helps to think about your development process and the different build types you'll need. It's very rare for a project to have a single build type and much more common for there to be at least three:

Development
> A development build is run by developers as they are working. This build should be as fast as possible so as not to interrupt developer productivity. Generally speaking, you want to prevent accidental errors and get the code into good testing shape so that developers can load it into the browser for hands-on testing. This build should take no more than 15 seconds, so you need to choose what you're doing carefully. If you're working on a web application, you may want to have a separate JavaScript development build that can be run independently of the overall web application build. This is also typically the default build.

Integration
> An automated build that is run on a regular schedule. These are sometimes run for each commit, but on large projects, they tend to be run on intervals for a few minutes. The integration build is responsible for finding problems in the entire system. Because it's automated, this build can take longer to complete but must be as thorough as possible. In some cases, the integration build is the last line of defense before pushing changes to production.

Release
> An on-demand build that is run only prior to a production push. This build's job is mostly to get the code into its final form so that it can be deployed. In theory, if the integration build did its job, then the release build shouldn't have errors. In practice, that's not always the case. The release build may be responsible for a few more tasks that could also cause errors before deployment.

Of course, your project have many more build types depending on your development process.

Your *build.xml* should always start out looking like this:

```
<project name="yourapp" default="build.dev">

    <!-- import properties -->
    <loadproperties srcfile="yourapp.properties" />

    <!-- define or import utility targets here -->

    <!-- initialization and cleanup -->
    <target name="init">
        <mkdir dir="${build.dir}"/>
    </target>
```

```
<target name="clean">
    <delete dir="${build.dir}"/>
</target>

<!-- main builds -->
<target name="build.dev">
</target>

<target name="build.int">
</target>

<target name="build.release">
</target>

</project>
```

Make sure to begin by importing the properties file(s) to get all of the data needed for the targets. Then, either include or import the utility targets such as those created in the preceding build system chapters. Sometimes it helps to keep the utility targets in one or more separate XML files, but ultimately it's up to you. After that, the `init` and `clean` targets round out the utility targets. The final section contains targets for each build type.

The Development Build

The development build is important to get correct because it affects every developer's workflow. Generally speaking, the goal of the development build is to get the code into the development environment as quickly as possible while still performing some sanity checks. Most development builds do just two things: validate the code and then concatenate the files. Because developers need the full source code for debugging, there is no point in minifying code at this point. Here's how the `build.dev` target looks:

```
<project name="yourapp" default="build.dev">

    <!-- omitted for clarity -->

    <!-- main builds -->
    <target name="build.dev" depends="clean,init,validate,concatenate">
    </target>

</project>
```

All of the primary build targets should look this simple, as they are simply tying together other targets in a particular order. The `build.dev` target specifies that it depends on the `clean`, `init`, `validate`, and `concatenate` targets to work. So running `ant build.dev` runs those four targets and does nothing else. As mentioned earlier, you should always ensure that you're starting with freshly built files, so be sure to remove old files first. Because the `concatenate` target also places the built files into the correct directory, the `build.dev` target is complete and should result in all the code being ready for use.

It's optional, but you might want to include testing in the development build or to let developers run `ant test` separately on their own. Keep in mind that testing takes more time due to the need to set up and tear down browser instances.

The Integration Build

The integration build runs automatically as part of a continuous integration (CI) system, so it has more steps to complete. Because this build is the main defense against errors, it should include as much validation and testing as possible. At a minimum, it should do everything the development build does plus unit testing. This is also a good location to place documentation generation so that other developers can see what changes have been made to the code. Here's a sample:

```
<project name="yourapp" default="build.dev">

    <!-- omitted for clarity -->

    <!-- main builds -->
    <target name="build.int depends="build.dev,minify,test,document">
    </target>

</project>
```

The `build.int` target first runs `build.dev` to complete the validation and concatenation of code. Next, the code is minified, then tested, and then documented. If this build breaks, it should cause the CI system to report an issue appropriately. Some systems sends out emails, others make visual changes to a stability dashboard. In any case, breaking the integration build is a matter that needs to be addressed quickly so that other developers aren't blocked.

 You may want to include documentation generation in its own automated build. The reason is that a failure to generate documentation doesn't necessarily mean that the code is broken. It might be that the document generator is broken for some reason. Once again, this largely depends on your development process and what you think is important enough to stop and fix before continuing.

The Release Build

The release build is the finish line of the development process. It is this build that ensures that code is fit for production. By the time code gets to the release build, it should have been validated and tested, both automatically and manually, and should therefore mostly be ready. In some cases, the only thing a release build needs to do is bake the files, inserting copyrights, version numbers, or other associated metadata. Here's an example:

```
<project name="yourapp" default="build.dev">

    <!-- omitted for clarity -->

    <!-- main builds -->
    <target name="build.release" depends="build.int,bake">
    </target>

</project>
```

The build.release target simply runs an integration build and then bakes the files. You might also want the release build to handle deploying of files to a server. In the case of JavaScript, this is typically done as part of a larger deployment build process for the web application or project rather than as part of the release build. However, you can certainly include a task to upload files to a server or perform other distribution tasks.

Another option for the release build is to simply take the output from the integration build and bake it before deployment. Doing so can save time and, assuming there were no errors in the integration build, ensure that you're deploying the exact same code that was tested. Once again, this choice is very project-specific, so be sure to discuss it with your team.

Using a CI System

Just using a build system is a good first step in creating a maintainable project. The next step is to integrate your build system into a CI system. CI systems run builds automatically based on certain actions or regular intervals. For instance, you might run a build once an hour to get all of the latest checked-in files deployed to an integration environment. If that fails, it may send emails to the developers asking them to fix any issues. Having a CI system is an important part of any good software project. Fortunately, there are some excellent free resources for CI.

Jenkins

Jenkins (*http://jenkins-ci.org/*) is one of the most widely used CI systems. It is a Java-based web application that is designed for managing multiple builds. It integrates with several source control repositories by default and can support almost any others through an extensive plugin library. Jenkins works natively with Ant as well as shell scripts, meaning that you can reuse any existing build scripts with Jenkins.

Setting up Jenkins is quite easy; just download the latest WAR file and start it:

```
java -jar jenkins.war
```

Jenkins starts up a web server accessible at *http://localhost:8080/*. Navigate to that location in your web browser, and you're ready to start creating build jobs.

A job is a collection of build steps to execute. Click the "New Job" link to create your first job. The next page asks you to select which type of job you'd like to create. If you're just using Ant for your build system, then select "Build a free-style software project." After creating the new job, you're taken to a configuration page.

There are some basic options on the configuration page, but the really interesting parts start lower on the page, with the section called "Build Triggers." This is where you decide how frequently the build should run. It can be triggered after another build finishes, on a timed schedule, or based on check-ins to source control. For your primary integration build, you'll probably want to kick off the build based on check-ins, so the last option works well. "Poll SCM" means that Jenkins will poll your source control system (as specified in the previous section). The poll format is the same as setting up a cron job on a Linux system, so @hourly works for checking source control each hour (see Figure 20-1).

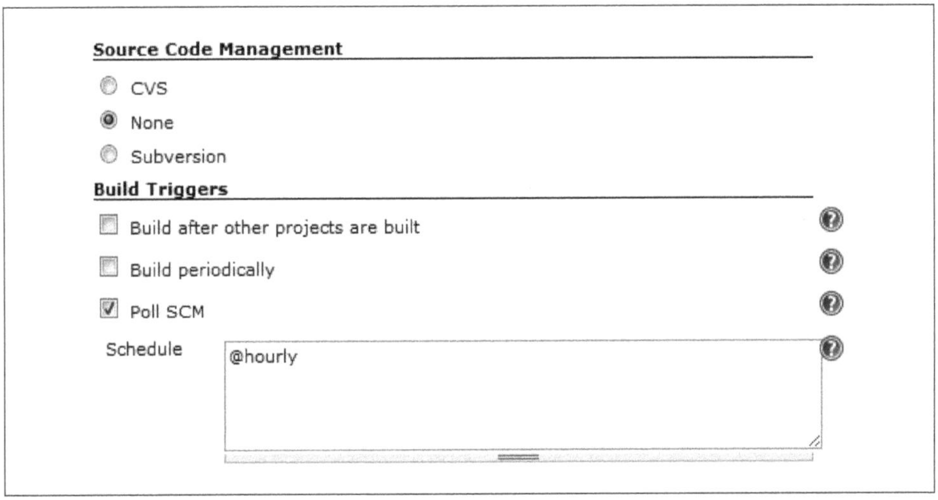

Figure 20-1. Jenkins build triggers

Next, you set up the job to execute one or more Ant targets. To do so, click the "Add Build Step" button to display a drop-down menu of options. Select "Invoke Ant." A new build step appears in the page asking you to specify the Ant targets to execute (see Figure 20-2).

If you're using Jenkins with source control, it will automatically find the *build.xml* file in your root directory, so you need specify only the Ant target name. If you're setting up the integration build, for example, then enter **build.int** into the textbox as in Figure 20-3.

If you're not using a *build.xml* file in the project root, or not using Jenkins with source control, then click on the "Advanced" button and you can specify the path to your *build.xml* file manually.

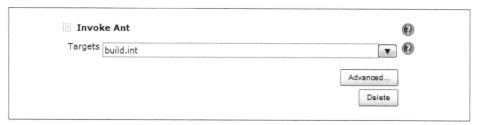

Build

Add build step ▾

| Execute Windows batch command |
| Execute shell |
| Invoke Ant |
| Invoke top-level Maven targets |

~~Archive the artifacts~~

☐ Build other projects ⑦

☐ Publish JUnit test result report ⑦

☐ Publish Javadoc

☐ Record fingerprints of files to track usage ⑦

☐ E-mail Notification ⑦

Save

Figure 20-2. Adding an Ant build step

▦ Invoke Ant ⑦

Targets build.int ▾ ⑦

Advanced...

Delete

Figure 20-3. Specifying an Ant target

After that, you can specify to send an email when the build fails. Jenkins allows you to specify the email address that should always be used for this notification, as well as for sending emails to the committers who broke the build (using source control to retrieve the email address). It's a good idea to always send an email when the build didn't succeed (see Figure 20-4).

Once you're done setting up email notifications, click "Save" at the bottom of the page to save the build job. Your build job will now execute once an hour; however, you can manually run the build at any time by going to Jenkins and clicking the "Build Now" link.

This is just a brief introduction to Jenkins and the power of continuous integration. There are many, many more things you can do with Jenkins, such as tracking the results of unit tests, publishing build logs, setting up dependent builds, and more. The Jenkins website is a great resource for learning more about the various options available.

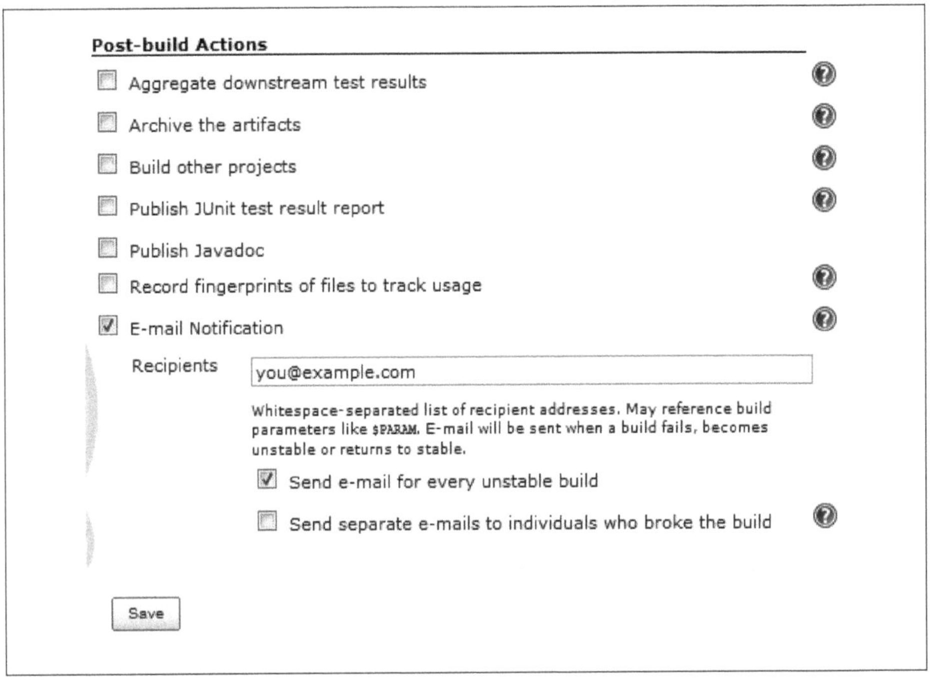

Figure 20-4. Configuring email notifications

Other CI Systems

CI is a popular area for research, so new solutions are coming out all the time. Here are some other free CI systems you may want to consider:

Continuum
    An Apache project for CI designed to work with Ant and Maven. It is available at *http://continuum.apache.org*.

BuildBot
    A Python-based build system targeted at engineers. It is available at *http://trac .buildbot.net*.

Cruise Control
    Another Java-based build system that works as a web application. Ruby and .NET ports also exist. It is available at *http://cruisecontrol.sourceforge.net*.

Gradle
    Uses a Groovy-based language on top of Ant and Maven for CI. A little bit difficult for nonprogrammers to work with. It is available at *http://www.gradle.org*.

JavaScript Style Guide

Programming language style guides are important for the long-term maintainability of software. This guide is based on the Code Conventions for the Java Programming Language (*http://%20java.sun.com/docs/codeconv/*) and Douglas Crockford's Code Conventions for the JavaScript Programming Language (*http://javascript.crockford.com/code.html*). Modifications have been made due to my personal experience and preferences.

Indentation

Each indentation level is made up of four spaces. Do not use tabs.

```
// Good
if (true) {
    doSomething();
}
```

Line Length

Each line should be no longer than 80 characters. If a line goes longer than 80 characters, it should be wrapped after an operator (comma, plus, etc.). The following line should be indented two levels (eight characters).

```
// Good
doSomething(argument1, argument2, argument3, argument4,
        argument5);

// Bad: Following line only indented four spaces
doSomething(argument1, argument2, argument3, argument4,
    argument5);

// Bad: Breaking before operator
doSomething(argument1, argument2, argument3, argument4
        , argument5);
```

Primitive Literals

Strings should always use double quotes (never single quotes) and should always appear on a single line. Never use a slash to create a new line in a string.

```
// Good
var name = "Nicholas";

// Bad: Single quotes
var name = 'Nicholas';

// Bad: Wrapping to second line
var longString = "Here's the story, of a man \
named Brady.";
```

Numbers should be written as decimal integers, e-notation integers, hexadecimal integers, or floating-point decimals with at least one digit before and one digit after the decimal point. Never use octal literals.

```
// Good
var count = 10;

// Good
var price = 10.0;
var price = 10.00;

// Good
var num = 0xA2;

// Good
var num = 1e23;

// Bad: Hanging decimal point
var price = 10.;

// Bad: Leading decimal point
var price = .1;

// Bad: Octal (base 8) is deprecated
var num = 010;
```

The special value null should be used only in the following situations:

- To initialize a variable that may later be assigned an object value
- To compare against an initialized variable that may or may not have an object value
- To pass into a function where an object is expected
- To return from a function where an object is expected

Examples:

```
// Good
var person = null;

// Good
```

```
function getPerson() {
    if (condition) {
        return new Person("Nicholas");
    } else {
        return null;
    }
}

// Good
var person = getPerson();
if (person !== null){
    doSomething();
}

// Bad: Testing against uninitialized variable
var person;
if (person != null){
    doSomething();
}

// Bad: Testing to see if an argument was passed
function doSomething(arg1, arg2, arg3, arg4){
    if (arg4 != null){
        doSomethingElse();
    }
}
```

Never use the special value undefined. To see if a variable has been defined, use the typeof operator:

```
// Good
if (typeof variable == "undefined") {
    // do something
}

// Bad: Using undefined literal
if (variable == undefined) {
    // do something
}
```

Operator Spacing

Operators with two operands must be preceded and followed by a single space to make the expression clear. Operators include assignments and logical operators.

```
// Good
var found = (values[i] === item);

// Good
if (found && (count > 10)) {
    doSomething();
}

// Good
```

```
for (i = 0; i < count; i++) {
    process(i);
}

// Bad: Missing spaces
var found = (values[i]===item);

// Bad: Missing spaces
if (found&&(count>10)) {
    doSomething();
}

// Bad: Missing spaces
for (i=0; i<count; i++) {
    process(i);
}
```

Parentheses Spacing

When parentheses are used, there should be no white space immediately after the opening paren or immediately before the closing paren.

```
// Good
var found = (values[i] === item);

// Good
if (found && (count > 10)) {
    doSomething();
}

// Good
for (i = 0; i < count; i++) {
    process(i);
}

// Bad: Extra space after opening paren
var found = ( values[i] === item);

// Bad: Extra space before closing paren
if (found && (count > 10) ) {
    doSomething();
}

// Bad: Extra space around argument
for (i = 0; i < count; i++) {
    process( i );
}
```

Object Literals

Object literals should have the following format:

- The opening brace should be on the same line as the containing statement.
- Each property-value pair should be indented one level with the first property appearing on the next line after the opening brace.
- Each property-value pair should have an unquoted property name, followed by a colon (no space preceding it), followed by the value.
- If the value is a function, it should wrap under the property name and should have a blank line both before and after the function.
- Additional empty lines may be inserted to group related properties or otherwise improve readability.
- The closing brace should be on a separate line.

Examples:

```
// Good
var object = {

    key1: value1,
    key2: value2,

    func: function() {
        // do something
    },

    key3: value3
};

// Bad: Improper indentation
var object = {
                key1: value1,
                key2: value2
            };

// Bad: Missing blank lines around function
var object = {

    key1: value1,
    key2: value2,
    func: function() {
        // do something
    },
    key3: value3
};
```

When an object literal is passed to a function, the opening brace should be on the same line as if the value is a variable. All other formatting rules listed earlier still apply.

```
// Good
doSomething({
    key1: value1,
    key2: value2
});

// Bad: All on one line
doSomething({ key1: value1, key2: value2 });
```

Comments

Make frequent use of comments to aid others in understanding your code. Use comments when:

- Code is difficult to understand.
- The code might be mistaken for an error.
- Browser-specific code is necessary but not obvious.
- Documentation generation is necessary for an object, method, or property (use appropriate documentation comments).

Single-Line Comments

Single-line comments should be used to documentation one line of code or a group of related lines of code. A single-line comment may be used in three ways:

- On a separate line, describing the code beneath it
- At the end of a line, describing the code before it
- On multiple lines, to comment out sections of code

When on a separate line, a single-line comment should be at the same indentation level as the code it describes and be preceded by a single line. Never use multiple single-line comments on consecutive lines; use a multiline comment instead.

```
// Good
if (condition){

    // if you made it here, then all security checks passed
    allowed();
}

// Bad: No empty line preceding comment
if (condition){
    // if you made it here, then all security checks passed
    allowed();
}

// Bad: Wrong indentation
if (condition){
```

```
    // if you made it here, then all security checks passed
        allowed();
    }

    // Bad: This should be a multiline comment
    // This next piece of code is quite difficult, so let me explain.
    // What you want to do is determine if the condition is true
    // and only then allow the user in. The condition is calculated
    // from several different functions and may change during the
    // lifetime of the session.
    if (condition){
        // if you made it here, then all security checks passed
        allowed();
    }
```

For single-line comments at the end of a line, ensure that there is at least one indentation level between the end of the code and the beginning of the comment:

```
    // Good
    var result = something + somethingElse;    // somethingElse will never be null

    // Bad: Not enough space between code and comment
    var result = something + somethingElse;// somethingElse will never be null
```

The only acceptable time to have multiple single-line comments on successive lines is to comment out large sections of code. Multiline comments should not be used for this purpose.

```
    // Good
    // if (condition){
    //    doSomething();
    //    thenDoSomethingElse();
    // }
```

Multiline Comments

Multiline comments should be used to document code that requires more explanation. Each multiline comment should have at least three lines:

1. The first line contains only the /* comment opening. No further text is allowed on this line.

2. The next line or lines have a * aligned with the * in the first line. Text is allowed on these lines.

3. The last line has the */ comment opening aligned with the preceding lines. No other text is allowed on this line.

The first line of multiline comments should be indented to the same level as the code it describes. Each subsequent line should have the same indentation plus one space (for proper alignment of the * characters). Each multiline comment should be preceded by one empty line.

```
// Good
if (condition){

    /*
     * if you made it here,
     * then all security checks passed
     */
    allowed();
}

// Bad: No empty line preceding comment
if (condition){
    /*
     * if you made it here,
     * then all security checks passed
     */
    allowed();
}

// Bad: Missing a space after asterisk
if (condition){

    /*
     *if you made it here,
     *then all security checks passed
     */
    allowed();
}

// Bad: Wrong indentation
if (condition){

/*
 * if you made it here,
 * then all security checks passed
 */
    allowed();
}

// Bad: Don't use multi-line comments for trailing comments
var result = something + somethingElse;    /*somethingElse will never be null*/
```

Comment Annotations

Comments may be used to annotate pieces of code with additional information. These annotations take the form of a single word followed by a colon. The acceptable annotations are:

TODO

Indicates that the code is not yet complete. Information about the next steps should be included.

HACK

Indicates that the code is using a shortcut. Information about why the hack is being used should be included. This may also indicate that it would be nice to come up with a better way to solve the problem.

XXX

Indicates that the code is problematic and should be fixed as soon as possible.

FIXME

Indicates that the code is problematic and should be fixed soon. Less important than XXX.

REVIEW

indicates that the code needs to be reviewed for potential changes.

These annotations may be used with either single-line or multiline comments and should follow the same formatting rules as the general comment type.

Examples:

```
// Good
// TODO: I'd like to find a way to make this faster
doSomething();

// Good
/*
 * HACK: Have to do this for IE. I plan on revisiting in
 * the future when I have more time. This probably should
 * get replaced before v1.2.
 */
if (document.all) {
    doSomething();
}

// Good
// REVIEW: Is there a better way to do this?
if (document.all) {
    doSomething();
}

// Bad: Annotation spacing is incorrect
// TODO : I'd like to find a way to make this faster
doSomething();

// Bad: Comment should be at the same indentation as code
    // REVIEW: Is there a better way to do this?
if (document.all) {
    doSomething();
}
```

Variable Declarations

All variables should be declared before they are used. Variable declarations should take place at the beginning of a function using a single `var` statement with one variable per line. All lines after the first should be indented one level so that the variable names line up. Variables should be initialized when declared if applicable, and the equals operator should be at a consistent indentation level. Initialized variables should come first followed by uninitialized variables.

```
// Good
var count    = 10,
    name     = "Nicholas",
    found    = false,
    empty;

// Bad: Improper initialization alignment
var count = 10,
    name = "Nicholas",
    found= false,
    empty;

// Bad: Incorrect indentation
var count    = 10,
name     = "Nicholas",
found    = false,
empty;

// Bad: Multiple declarations on one line
var count    = 10, name = "Nicholas",
    found    = false, empty;

// Bad: Uninitialized variables first
var empty,
    count    = 10,
    name     = "Nicholas",
    found    = false;

// Bad: Multiple var statements
var count    = 10,
    name     = "Nicholas";

var found    = false,
    empty;
```

Always declare variables. Implied globals should not be used.

Function Declarations

Functions should be declared before they are used. When a function is not a method (that is, not attached to an object), it should be defined using the function declaration format (not function expression format or using the `Function` constructor). There

---

should be no space between the function name and the opening parenthesis. There should be one space between the closing parenthesis and the left brace. The left brace should be on the same line as the `function` keyword. There should be no space after the opening parenthesis or before the closing parenthesis. Named arguments should have a space after the comma but not before it. The function body should be indented one level.

```
// Good
function doSomething(arg1, arg2) {
    return arg1 + arg2;
}

// Bad: Improper spacing of first line
function doSomething (arg1, arg2){
    return arg1 + arg2;
}

// Bad: Function expression
var doSomething = function(arg1, arg2) {
    return arg1 + arg2;
};

// Bad: Left brace on wrong line
function doSomething(arg1, arg2)
{
    return arg1 + arg2;
}

// Bad: Using Function constructor
var doSomething = new Function("arg1", "arg2", "return arg1 + arg2");
```

Functions declared inside of other functions should be declared immediately after the `var` statement.

```
// Good
function outer() {

    var count   = 10,
        name    = "Nicholas",
        found   = false,
        empty;

    function inner() {
        // code
    }

    // code that uses inner()
}

// Bad: Inner function declared before variables
function outer() {

    function inner() {
        // code
```

```
    }

    var count    = 10,
        name     = "Nicholas",
        found    = false,
        empty;

    // code that uses inner()
}
```

Anonymous functions may be used for assignment of object methods or as arguments
to other functions. There should be no space between the `function` keyword and the
opening parenthesis.

```
// Good
object.method = function() {
    // code
};

// Bad: Incorrect spacing
object.method = function () {
    // code
};
```

Immediately invoked functions should surround the entire function call with parentheses.

```
// Good
var value = (function() {

    // function body

    return {
        message: "Hi"
    }
}());

// Bad: No parentheses around function call
var value = function() {

    // function body

    return {
        message: "Hi"
    }
}();

// Bad: Improper parentheses placement
var value = (function() {

    // function body

    return {
        message: "Hi"
    }
})();
```

Naming

Care should be taken to name variables and functions properly. Names should be limited to alphanumeric characters and, in some cases, the underscore character. Do not use the dollar sign ($) or backslash (\) characters in any names.

Variable names should be formatted in camel case with the first letter lowercase and the first letter of each subsequent word uppercase. The first word of a variable name should be a noun (not a verb) to avoid confusion with functions. Do not use underscores in variable names.

```
// Good
var accountNumber = "8401-1";

// Bad: Begins with uppercase letter
var AccountNumber = "8401-1";

// Bad: Begins with verb
var getAccountNumber = "8401-1";

// Bad: Uses underscore
var account_number = "8401-1";
```

Function names should also be formatted using camel case. The first word of a function name should be a verb (not a noun) to avoid confusion with variables. Do not use underscores in function names.

```
// Good
function doSomething() {
    // code
}

// Bad: Begins with uppercase letter
function DoSomething() {
    // code
}

// Bad: Begins with noun
function car() {
    // code
}

// Bad: Uses underscores
function do_something() {
    // code
}
```

Constructor functions—functions used with the new operator to create new objects—should be formatted in camel case but must begin with an uppercase letter. Constructor function names should begin with a nonverb, because new is the action of creating an object instance.

```
// Good
function MyObject() {
    // code
}

// Bad: Begins with lowercase letter
function myObject() {
    // code
}

// Bad: Uses underscores
function My_Object() {
    // code
}

// Bad: Begins with verb
function getMyObject() {
    // code
}
```

Variables that act as constants (values that won't be changed) should be formatted using all uppercase letters with words separated by a single underscore.

```
// Good
var TOTAL_COUNT = 10;

// Bad: Camel case
var totalCount = 10;

// Bad: Mixed case
var total_COUNT = 10;
```

Object properties follow the same naming conventions as variables. Object methods follow the same naming conventions as functions. If a property or method is meant to be private, then it should be prefixed with an underscore character.

```
// Good
var object = {
    _count: 10,

    _getCount: function () {
        return this._count;
    }
};
```

Strict Mode

Strict mode should be used only inside of functions, never globally.

```
// Bad: Global strict mode
"use strict";

function doSomething() {
    // code
}
```

```
// Good
function doSomething() {
    "use strict";

    // code
}
```

If you want strict mode to apply to multiple functions without needing to write "use strict" multiple times, use immediate function invocation:

```
// Good
(function() {
    "use strict";

    function doSomething() {
        // code
    }

    function doSomethingElse() {
        // code
    }

}());
```

Assignments

When assigning a value to a variable, use parentheses around a right-side expression that contains a comparison.

```
// Good
var flag = (i < count);

// Bad: Missing parentheses
var flag = i < count;
```

Equality Operators

Use === and !== instead of == and != to avoid type coercion errors.

```
// Good
var same = (a === b);

// Bad: Using ==
var same = (a == b);
```

Ternary Operator

The ternary operator should be used only for assigning values conditionally and never as a shortcut for an if statement.

```
// Good
var value = condition ? value1 : value2;

// Bad: no assignment, should be an if statement
condition ? doSomething() : doSomethingElse();
```

Statements

Simple Statements

Each line should contain at most one statement. All simple statements should end with a semicolon (;).

```
// Good
count++;
a = b;

// Bad: Multiple statements on one line
count++; a = b;
```

return Statement

A `return` statement with a value should not use parentheses unless they make the return value more obvious in some way. Example:

```
return;
```

```
return collection.size();
```

```
return (size > 0 ? size : defaultSize);
```

Compound Statements

Compound statements are lists of statements enclosed inside of braces.

- The enclosed statements should be indented one more level than the compound statement.
- The opening brace should be at the end of the line that begins the compound statement; the closing brace should begin a line and be indented to the beginning of the compound statement.
- Braces are used around all statements, even single statements, when they are part of a control structure, such as an `if` or `for` statement. This convention makes it easier to add statements without accidentally introducing bugs by forgetting to add braces.
- The statement beginning keyword, such as `if`, should be followed by one space, and the opening brace should be preceded by a space.

if Statement

The if class of statements should have the following form:

```
if (condition) {
    statements
}

if (condition) {
    statements
} else {
    statements
}

if (condition) {
    statements
} else if (condition) {
    statements
} else {
    statements
}
```

It is never permissible to omit the braces in any part of an if statement.

```
// Good
if (condition) {
    doSomething();
}

// Bad: Improper spacing
if(condition){
    doSomething();
}

// Bad: Missing braces
if (condition)
    doSomething();

// Bad: All on one line
if (condition) { doSomething(); }

// Bad: All on one line without braces
if (condition) doSomething();
```

for Statement

The for class of statements should have the following form:

```
for (initialization; condition; update) {
    statements
}

for (variable in object) {
    statements
}
```

Variables should not be declared in the initialization section of a for statement.

```
// Good
var i,
    len;

for (i=0, len=10; i < len; i++) {
    // code
}

// Bad: Variables declared during initialization
for (var i=0, len=10; i < len; i++) {
    // code
}

// Bad: Variables declared during initialization
for (var prop in object) {
    // code
}
```

When using a for-in statement, double-check if you need to use hasOwnProperty() to filter out object members.

while Statement

The while class of statements should have the following form:

```
while (condition) {
    statements
}
```

do Statement

The do class of statements should have the following form:

```
do {
    statements
} while (condition);
```

Note the use of a semicolon as the final part of this statement. There should be a space before and after the while keyword.

switch Statement

The switch class of statements should have the following form:

```
switch (expression) {
    case expression:
        statements

    default:
        statements
}
```

Each case is indented one level under the switch. Each case after the first, including default, should be preceded by a single empty line.

Each group of statements (except the default) should end with break, return, throw, or a comment indicating fall-through.

```
// Good
switch (value) {
    case 1:
        /* falls through */

    case 2:
        doSomething();
        break;

    case 3:
        return true;

    default:
        throw new Error("This shouldn't happen.");
}
```

If a switch doesn't have a default case, then it should be indicated with a comment.

```
// Good
switch (value) {
    case 1:
        /*falls through*/

    case 2:
        doSomething();
        break;

    case 3:
        return true;

    // no default
}
```

try Statement

The try class of statements should have the following form:

```
try {
    statements
} catch (variable) {
    statements
}

try {
    statements
} catch (variable) {
    statements
} finally {
```

```
            statements
        }
```

White Space

Blank lines improve readability by setting off sections of code that are logically related.

Two blank lines should always be used in the following circumstances:

- Between sections of a source file
- Between class and interface definitions

One blank line should always be used in the following circumstances:

- Between methods
- Between the local variables in a method and its first statement
- Before a multiline or single-line comment
- Between logical sections inside a method to improve readability

Blank spaces should be used in the following circumstances:

- A keyword followed by a parenthesis should be separated by a space.
- A blank space should appear after commas in argument lists.
- All binary operators except dot (.) should be separated from their operands by spaces. Blank spaces should never separate unary operators such as unary minus, increment (++), and decrement (--) from their operands.
- The expressions in a `for` statement should be separated by blank spaces.

Things to Avoid

- Never use the primitive wrapper types, such as `String`, to create new objects.
- Never use `eval()`.
- Never use the `with` statement. This statement isn't available in strict mode and likely won't be available in future ECMAScript editions.

JavaScript Tools

Build Tools

Though many build tools are not JavaScript-specific, they can still be quite useful in managing your large JavaScript projects:

Ant (http://ant.apache.org)
: My preferred build tool for JavaScript projects. A Java-based build system.

Buildy (https://github.com/mosen/buildy)
: A Node.js-based build system with built-in support for tasks related to JavaScript and CSS.

Gmake (http://www.gnu.org/s/make/)
: An older build tool that's still popular among Unix devotees. Gmake is used by jQuery.

Grunt (https://github.com/cowboy/grunt)
: A Node.js-based build system with built-in support for JavaScript-related tasks like minification and concatenation.

Jammit (http://documentcloud.github.com/jammit/)
: A Ruby-based asset packager that handles minification, validation, and more.

Jasy (https://github.com/zynga/jasy)
: A Python-based build system.

Rake (http://rake.rubyforge.org/)
: A utility similar to Gmake written in Ruby. Projects that use Sass, a popular CSS preprocessor, tend to use Rake.

Sprockets (http://getsprockets.org)
: A Rack-based build system.

Documentation Generators

Documentation generators create documentation from comments placed in source code:

Docco (http://jashkenas.github.com/docco/)
> A side-by-side documentation generator, showing documents alongside code. Written in CoffeeScript.

Dojo Documentation Tools (http://dojotoolkit.org/reference-guide/util/doctools.html)
> The official documentation generator of Dojo. Written in PHP.

JoDoc (https://github.com/azakus/jodoc-js)
> A JavaScript documentation generator that uses Markdown syntax. Written in JavaScript.

JSDoc ToolKit (http://code.google.com/p/jsdoc-toolkit/)
> A Java-based documentation generator. One of the most frequently used documentation generators.

Natural Docs (http://www.naturaldocs.org)
> A general-purpose documentation generator that works with multiple languages. Written in Perl.

NDoc (https://github.com/nodeca/ndoc)
> A JavaScript port of PDoc.

PDoc (http://pdoc.org/)
> The official documentation generator of Prototype. Written in Ruby.

YUI Doc (http://yuilibrary.com/projects/yuidoc)
> The YUI documentation generator. Written in JavaScript.

Linting Tools

Linting tools help identify problematic styles and patterns in your code:

JSLint (http://jslint.com)
> Douglas Crockford's code-quality tool.

JSHint (http://jshint.com)
> A fork of JSLint with more configurable options.

Minification Tools

Minification tools make JavaScript files smaller by removing unnecessary comments and white space and perhaps performing other code optimization.

Closure Compiler (http://code.google.com/closure/compiler/)
> Google's Java-based JavaScript minifier.

UglifyJS (https://github.com/mishoo/UglifyJS)
   A Node.js-based JavaScript minifier.

YUI Compressor (http://yuilibrary.com/projects/yuicompressor)
   A Java-based JavaScript and CSS minifier.

Testing Tools

Testing tools allow you to write and execute tests that verify the behavior of your code:

Jasmine (http://pivotal.github.com/jasmine/)
   A behavior-driven JavaScript testing framework.

JsTestDriver (http://code.google.com/p/js-test-driver/)
   The Google unit test framework, which includes automated browser testing.

PhantomJS (http://www.phantomjs.org)
   A headless WebKit browser designed for testing. Can be used with QUnit and Jasmine by default and others through a driver system.

QUnit (http://docs.jquery.com/QUnit)
   The jQuery unit testing framework.

Selenium (http://seleniumhq.com)
   A functional testing framework that can be used for browser testing.

Yeti (http://yuilibrary.com/projects/yeti)
   A test harness for JavaScript testing in browsers.

YUI Test (http://yuilibrary.com/projects/yuitest)
   The YUI unit testing framework.

Index

Symbols

!= operator, 45
!== operator, 46, 84
== operator, 45
=== operator, 46, 84

A

Adams, Douglas, 125
addClass() function, 98
addEventListener() function, 58
addItem() function, 62
AMD (Asynchronous Module Definition)
    modules, 75–76
Android Code Style Guidelines for
    Contributors, 9
anonymous functions, 43
Ant build tool
    about, 133
    baking files, 148–149
    build-time compression, 158
    build.xml file, 133–134
    Buildr project, 137
    concatenation, 145
    creating build directory, 177
    installing, 133
    properties, 136
    running the build, 134
    target dependencies, 135
Apache web server, 158
application logic, 80
<apply> task
    about, 140
    executable attribute, 156
    failonerror property, 142

    parallel attribute, 141, 163
    YUI Compressor and, 153
array literals
    about, 19
    square brackets and, 19
Array object
    forEach() method, 106, 111
    isArray() method, 88
    length property, 108
Array reference type, 85, 88
ASI (automatic semicolon insertion), 7, 9
Asynchronous Module Definition (AMD)
    modules, 75–76
automated testing
    about, 167
    JsTestDriver utility, 173–175
    PhantomJS engine, 172–173
    Yeti tool, 171
    YUI Test Selenium Server, 167–170
automatic semicolon insertion (ASI), 7, 9
automation
    advantages and disadvantages, 125
    Ant build tool, 133–137
    assembling final system, 177–184
    automated testing, 167–175
    baking files, 148–149
    code validation, 139–143
    compression process, 157–160
    concatenation, 145–147
    documentation generators, 161–165
    file and directory structure, 127–132
    minification process, 151–157

B

baking files, 148–149

We'd like to hear your suggestions for improving our indexes. Send email to *index@oreilly.com*.

<property> element
   about, 136
   name attribute, 136
   value attribute, 136
Props2Js tool, 94
prototypal inheritance, 108
Prototype library, 105

Q

QUnit tests, 172
quotation marks, 15

R

RangeError object, 100
reference values
   about, 85
   detecting, 85–87
   detecting arrays, 88
   detecting functions, 87
ReferenceError object, 70, 100
release builds, 178, 180
<replaceregexp> task
   about, 148
   byline attribute, 149
   flags attribute, 149
   match attribute, 149
   replace attribute, 149
require() function, 76
RequireJS module loader, 76
return statement, 200
REVIEW annotation, 193
Rhino engine, 140
runtime compression, 157

S

<script> element
   embedding JavaScript in HTML, 58, 59
   language attribute, 158
   text property, 62
   type property, 62, 63
scripts
   naming collisions in, 68
   PhantomJS engine support, 172
   strict mode, 44
   zero-global approach, 76
semicolons
   terminating statements with, 7
   variable declarations and, 69

setInterval() function, 48
setTimeout() function, 48, 119
shims (polyfills), 111
single-line comments, 21–22, 190
Souder, Steve, 55
spaces for indentation levels, 6
spacing rules
   block statements, 31
   function calls, 42
   operators, 187
   parentheses, 188
   white space, 204
SproutCore Style Guide
   brace alignment, 30
   equality operators, 47
   function call spacing, 43
   indentation levels, 7
   naming conventions, 11, 13
   statements and curly braces, 29
   variable declarations, 40
square brackets, array literals and, 19
src directory, 128, 139, 164
<srcfile> element, 141, 153
statements, 31
   (see also specific statements)
   about, 200
   blank lines and, 11
   block statement spacing, 31
   brace alignment, 30
   compound, 200
   curly braces and, 29
   terminating, 7
storing configuration data, 93–94
strict mode
   about, 198
   avoiding accidental globals, 70
   immediate function invocation, 44
   preventing object modification, 114
   with statement and, 35
String.toUpperCase() method, 49
strings
   about, 14
   multiline, 15
   as primitive types, 48, 83, 186
   quotation marks and, 15
   typeof operator and, 84
style guidelines
   about, 1
   basic formatting, 5–19

About the Author

Nicholas C. Zakas is a front-end consultant, author, and speaker. He worked at Yahoo! for almost five years, where he was front-end tech lead for the Yahoo! home page and a contributor to the YUI library. He is the author of *Professional JavaScript for Web Developers* (Wrox, 2012), *Professional Ajax* (Wrox, 2007), and *High Performance Java-Script (http://shop.oreilly.com/product/9780596802806.do)* (O'Reilly, 2010). Nicholas is a strong advocate for development best practices including progressive enhancement, accessibility, performance, scalability, and maintainability. He blogs regularly at *http://www.nczonline.net/* and can be found on Twitter via @slicknet.

Colophon

The animal on the cover of *Maintainable JavaScript* is a Greek tortoise.

Greek tortoises (*Testudo graeca*), also known as spur-thighed tortoises, are currently divided into at least 20 known subspecies, and as such vary greatly in size, weight, and color. They inhabit areas of North Africa, southern Europe, and southwest Asia, where they tend to prefer hot, arid regions; however, they can also be found on mountain steppes and seashore dunes. Their genetic richness makes their classification difficult and results largely from their crossbreeding; tortoises from different groups often mate, resulting in offspring of widely varying colors and sizes. For this reason, one of the best ways to identify a particular specimen is to know where it came from.

Greek tortoises range in size from 8 inches to around 12 inches. The "spurs" on their thighs refer to the two small tubercles that sit on either side of the tail, and in general, their carapace, or upper shell, is oblong rectangular. They're also generally characterized by large scales on their front legs; flecks on the spine and rib plates, with a larger, dark fleck on the underside; and an upper shell that's undivided over the tail.

Greek tortoises' mating instincts kick in immediately after they awake from hibernation. One or two weeks before egg-laying takes place, the tortoises move around their habitat—digging in, tasting, and smelling the dirt—in order to find the ideal egg-laying area. One or two days before laying eggs, the female Greek tortoise becomes aggressive in order to establish dominance in the community so that her eggs will not be disturbed. Their average lifespan is 50 years.

The cover image is from Cassell's *Natural History*. The cover font is Adobe ITC Garamond. The text font is Linotype Birka; the heading font is Adobe Myriad Condensed; and the code font is LucasFont's TheSansMonoCondensed.

Learn from experts.
Find the answers you need.

Sign up for a **10-day free trial** to get **unlimited access** to all of the content on Safari, including Learning Paths, interactive tutorials, and curated playlists that draw from thousands of ebooks and training videos on a wide range of topics, including data, design, DevOps, management, business—and much more.

Start your free trial at:
oreilly.com/safari

(No credit card required.)

Lightning Source UK Ltd.
Milton Keynes UK
UKHW031123140721
387152UK00004B/144